ELECTI

REVISED 2008 EDITION

by
GEORGE V. HART
and
SAMMIE HART

WILLIAM C. BUCHANAN
Editor

DISTRIBUTED BY:
Burleson Distributing Corp. · 3501 Oak Forest Drive · Houston, Texas 77018
(713) 956-6666 · (800) 531-1660 · Fax (713) 956-6576
E-mail: uglys@uglys.net
Website: www.uglys.net

TABLE OF CONTENTS

TABLE OF CONTENTS (continued)

TABLE OF CONTENTS (continued)

OHM'S LAW

***The rate of the flow of the current is equal to
electromotive force divided by resistance.***

I = **Intensity of Current = Amperes**
E = **Electromotive Force = Volts**
R = **Resistance = Ohms**
P = **Power = Watts**

The three basic Ohm's law formulas are:

$$I = \frac{E}{R} \qquad\qquad R = \frac{E}{I} \qquad\qquad E = I \times R$$

Below is a chart containing the formulas related to Ohm's law.
To use the chart, from the center circle, select the value you need to
find, I (Amps), R (Ohms), E (Volts) or P (Watts). Then select the
formula containing the values you know from the corresponding chart
quadrant.

Example:
An electric appliance is rated at 1200 Watts, and is connected to 120
Volts. How much current will it draw?

Amperes $= \dfrac{\textbf{Watts}}{\textbf{Volts}}$ $\qquad$ $I = \dfrac{P}{E}$ $\qquad$ $I = \dfrac{1200}{120} = 10\ A$

What is the Resistance of the same appliance?

Ohms $= \dfrac{\textbf{Volts}}{\textbf{Amperes}}$ $\qquad$ $R = \dfrac{E}{I}$ $\qquad$ $R = \dfrac{120}{10} = 12\ \Omega$

OHM'S LAW

In the preceding example, we know the following values:

I = amps = 10 R = ohms = 12Ω
E = volts = 120 P = watts = 1200

We can now see how the twelve formulas in the Ohm's Law chart can be applied.

$$\text{AMPS} = \sqrt{\frac{\text{WATTS}}{\text{OHMS}}} \qquad I = \sqrt{\frac{P}{R}} = \sqrt{\frac{1200}{12}} = \sqrt{100} = 10A$$

$$\text{AMPS} = \frac{\text{WATTS}}{\text{VOLTS}} \qquad I = \frac{P}{E} = \frac{1200}{120} = 10A$$

$$\text{AMPS} = \frac{\text{VOLTS}}{\text{OHMS}} \qquad I = \frac{E}{R} = \frac{120}{12} = 10A$$

$$\text{WATTS} = \frac{\text{VOLTS}^2}{\text{OHMS}} \qquad P = \frac{E^2}{R} = \frac{120^2}{12} = \frac{14,400}{12} = 1200W$$

$$\text{WATTS} = \text{VOLTS} \times \text{AMPS} \qquad P = E \times I = 120 \times 10 = 1200W$$

$$\text{WATTS} = \text{AMPS}^2 \times \text{OHMS} \qquad P = I^2 \times R = 100 \times 12 = 1200W$$

$$\text{VOLTS} = \sqrt{\text{WATTS} \times \text{OHMS}} \qquad E = \sqrt{P \times R} = \sqrt{1200 \times 12} = \sqrt{14,400} = 120V$$

$$\text{VOLTS} = \text{AMPS} \times \text{OHMS} \qquad E = I \times R = 10 \times 12 = 120V$$

$$\text{VOLTS} = \frac{\text{WATTS}}{\text{AMPS}} \qquad E = \frac{P}{I} = \frac{1200}{10} = 120V$$

$$\text{OHMS} = \frac{\text{VOLTS}^2}{\text{WATTS}} \qquad R = \frac{E^2}{P} = \frac{120^2}{1,200} = \frac{14,400}{1,200} = 12\Omega$$

$$\text{OHMS} = \frac{\text{WATTS}}{\text{AMPS}^2} \qquad R = \frac{P}{I^2} = \frac{1200}{100} = 12\Omega$$

$$\text{OHMS} = \frac{\text{VOLTS}}{\text{AMPS}} \qquad R = \frac{E}{I} = \frac{120}{10} = 12\Omega$$

SERIES CIRCUITS

A SERIES CIRCUIT is a circuit that has only one path through which the electrons may flow.

RULE 1: The total current in a series circuit is equal to the current in any other part of the circuit.

$$\text{TOTAL CURRENT} \quad I_T = I_1 = I_2 = I_3, \text{ etc.}$$

RULE 2: The total voltage in a series circuit is equal to the sum of the voltages across all parts of the circuit.

$$\text{TOTAL VOLTAGE} \quad E_T = E_1 + E_2 + E_3, \text{ etc.}$$

RULE 3: The total resistance of a series circuit is equal to the sum of the resistances of all the parts of the circuit

$$\text{TOTAL RESISTANCE} \quad R_T = R_1 + R_2 + R_3, \text{ etc.}$$

FORMULAS FROM OHM'S LAW

$$\text{AMPERES} = \frac{\text{VOLTS}}{\text{RESISTANCE}} \qquad \text{OR} \qquad I = \frac{E}{R}$$

$$\text{RESISTANCE} = \frac{\text{VOLTS}}{\text{AMPERES}} \qquad \text{OR} \qquad R = \frac{E}{I}$$

$$\text{VOLTS} = \text{AMPERES} \times \text{RESISTANCE} \qquad \text{OR} \qquad E = I \times R$$

EXAMPLE: Find the total voltage, total current, and total resistance of the following series circuit.

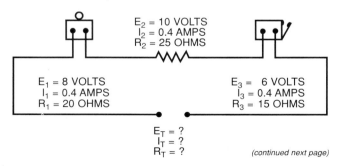

$E_2 = 10$ VOLTS
$I_2 = 0.4$ AMPS
$R_2 = 25$ OHMS

$E_1 = 8$ VOLTS
$I_1 = 0.4$ AMPS
$R_1 = 20$ OHMS

$E_3 = 6$ VOLTS
$I_3 = 0.4$ AMPS
$R_3 = 15$ OHMS

$E_T = ?$
$I_T = ?$
$R_T = ?$

(continued next page)

SERIES CIRCUITS

$$E_T = E_1 + E_2 + E_3$$
$$= 8 + 10 + 6$$
$$E_T = 24 \text{ VOLTS}$$

$$I_T = I_1 = I_2 = I_3$$
$$= 0.4 = 0.4 = 0.4$$
$$I_T = 0.4 \text{ AMPS}$$

$$R_T = R_1 + R_2 + R_3$$
$$= 20 + 25 + 15$$
$$R_T = 60 \text{ OHMS}$$

EXAMPLE: Find E_T, E_1, E_3, I_T, I_1, I_2, I_4, R_T, R_2, AND R_4. Remember that the total current in a series circuit is equal to the current in any other part of the circuit.

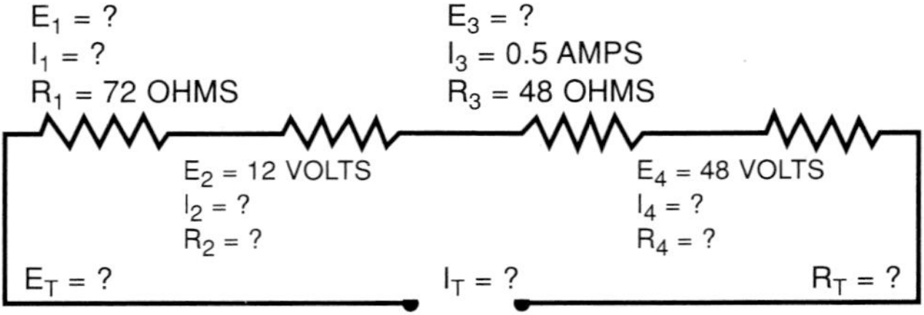

$E_1 = ?$
$I_1 = ?$
$R_1 = 72 \text{ OHMS}$

$E_3 = ?$
$I_3 = 0.5 \text{ AMPS}$
$R_3 = 48 \text{ OHMS}$

$E_2 = 12 \text{ VOLTS}$
$I_2 = ?$
$R_2 = ?$

$E_4 = 48 \text{ VOLTS}$
$I_4 = ?$
$R_4 = ?$

$E_T = ?$ $I_T = ?$ $R_T = ?$

$$I_T = I_1 = I_2 = I_3 = I_4$$
$$I_T = I_1 = I_2 = 0.5 = I_4$$
$$0.5 = 0.5 = 0.5 = 0.5 = 0.5$$
$$I_T = 0.5 \text{ AMPS} \quad I_2 = 0.5 \text{ AMPS}$$
$$I_1 = 0.5 \text{ AMPS} \quad I_4 = 0.5 \text{ AMPS}$$

$$E_1 = I_1 \times R_1$$
$$= 0.5 \times 72$$
$$E_1 = 36 \text{ VOLTS}$$

$$E_T = E_1 + E_2 + E_3 + E_4$$
$$= 36 + 12 + 24 + 48$$
$$E_T = 120 \text{ VOLTS}$$

$$E_3 = I_3 \times R_3$$
$$= 0.5 \times 48$$
$$E_3 = 24 \text{ VOLTS}$$

$$R_T = R_1 + R_2 + R_3 + R_4$$
$$= 72 + 24 + 48 + 96$$
$$R_T = 240 \text{ OHMS}$$

$$R_2 = \frac{E_2}{I_2} = \frac{12}{0.5}$$
$$R_2 = 24 \text{ OHMS}$$

$$R_4 = \frac{E_4}{I_4} = \frac{48}{0.5}$$
$$R_4 = 96 \text{ OHMS}$$

PARALLEL CIRCUITS

A PARALLEL CIRCUIT is a circuit that has more than one path through which the electrons may flow.

RULE 1: The total current in a parallel circuit is equal to the sum of the currents in all the branches of the circuit.

TOTAL CURRENT $I_T = I_1 + I_2 + I_3$, etc.

RULE 2: The total voltage across any branch in parallel is equal to the voltage across any other branch and is also equal to the total voltage.

TOTAL VOLTAGE $E_T = E_1 = E_2 = E_3$, etc.

RULE 3: The total resistance of a parallel circuit is found by applying OHM'S LAW to the total values of the circuit.

$$\text{TOTAL RESISTANCE} = \frac{\text{TOTAL VOLTAGE}}{\text{TOTAL AMPERES}} \quad \text{OR} \quad R_T = \frac{E_T}{I_T}$$

Example: Find the total current, total voltage, and total resistance of the following parallel circuit.

$E_1 = 120$ V	$E_2 = 120$ V	$E_3 = 120$ V
$I_1 = 2$ AMP	$I_2 = 1.5$ AMP	$I_3 = 1$ AMP
$R_1 = 60$ OHMS	$R_2 = 80$ OHMS	$R_3 = 120$ OHMS

$$
\begin{aligned}
I_T &= I_1 + I_2 + I_3 \\
&= 2 + 1.5 + 1 \\
I_T &= 4.5 \text{ AMPS}
\end{aligned}
\qquad
\begin{aligned}
E_T &= E_1 = E_2 = E_3 \\
&= 120 = 120 = 120 \\
E_T &= 120 \text{ VOLTS}
\end{aligned}
$$

$$R_T = \frac{E_T}{I_T} = \frac{120 \text{ VOLTS}}{4.5 \text{ AMPS}} = 26.66 \text{ OHMS RESISTANCE}$$

NOTE: In a parallel circuit, the total resistance is always less than the resistance of any branch. If the branches of a parallel circuit have the same resistance, then each will draw the same current. If the branches of a parallel circuit have different resistances, then each will draw a different current. In either series or parallel circuits, the larger the resistance, the smaller the current drawn.

PARALLEL CIRCUITS

To determine the total resistance in a parallel circuit when the total current and total voltage are unknown:

$$\frac{1}{\text{TOTAL RESISTANCE}} = \frac{1}{R_1} + \frac{1}{R_2} + \frac{1}{R_3} \quad \textbf{AND ETC.}$$

EXAMPLE: Find the total resistance of the following circuit:

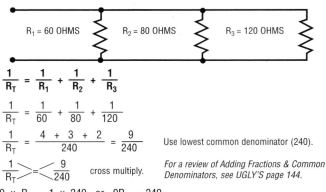

$$\frac{1}{R_T} = \frac{1}{R_1} + \frac{1}{R_2} + \frac{1}{R_3}$$

$$\frac{1}{R_T} = \frac{1}{60} + \frac{1}{80} + \frac{1}{120}$$

$$\frac{1}{R_T} = \frac{4 + 3 + 2}{240} = \frac{9}{240} \qquad \text{Use lowest common denominator (240).}$$

$$\frac{1}{R_T} >\!\!<\frac{9}{240} \quad \text{cross multiply.}$$

For a review of Adding Fractions & Common Denominators, see UGLY'S page 144.

$9 \times R_T = 1 \times 240$ or $9R_T = 240$
divide both sides of the equation by 9
$R_T = 26.66$ OHMS RESISTANCE

NOTE: The total resistance of a number of EQUAL resistors in parallel is equal to the resistance of one resistor divided by the number of resistors.

$$\textbf{TOTAL RESISTANCE} = \frac{\textbf{RESISTANCE OF ONE RESISTOR}}{\textbf{NUMBER OF RESISTORS IN CIRCUIT}}$$

(continued next page)

PARALLEL CIRCUITS

FORMULA: $$R_T = \frac{R}{N}$$

EXAMPLE: Find the total resistance

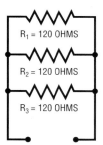

R_1 = 120 OHMS

R_2 = 120 OHMS

R_3 = 120 OHMS

There are three resistors in parallel. Each has a value of 120 OHMS resistance. According to the formula, if we divide the resistance of any one of the resistors by three, we will obtain the total resistance of the circuit.

$$R_T = \frac{R}{N} \quad OR \quad R_T = \frac{120}{3}$$

TOTAL RESISTANCE = 40 OHMS.

NOTE: To find the total resistance of only two resistors in parallel, multiply the resistances, and then divide the product by the sum of the resistors.

FORMULA: TOTAL RESISTANCE $= \dfrac{R_1 \times R_2}{R_1 + R_2}$

EXAMPLE:

R_1 = 40 OHMS

R_2 = 80 OHMS

$$R_T = \frac{R_1 \times R_2}{R_1 + R_2}$$

$$= \frac{40 \times 80}{40 + 80}$$

$$R_T = \frac{3200}{120} = 26.66 \text{ OHMS}$$

COMBINATION CIRCUITS

In combination circuits, we combine series circuits with parallel circuits. Combination circuits make it possible to obtain the different voltages of series circuits, and the different currents of parallel circuits.

EXAMPLE 1. PARALLEL-SERIES CIRCUIT:
Solve for all missing values.

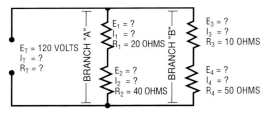

TO SOLVE:
1. Find the total resistance of each branch. Both branches are simple series circuits, so

   $R_1 + R_2 = R_A$
   20 + 40 = 60 OHMS total resistance of branch "A"

   $R_3 + R_4 = R_B$
   10 + 50 = 60 OHMS total resistance of branch "B"

2. Re-draw the circuit, combining resistors ($R_1 + R_2$) and ($R_3 + R_4$) so that each branch will have only one resistor.

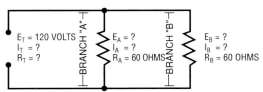

(continued next page)

COMBINATION CIRCUITS

NOTE: We now have a simple parallel circuit, so

$$E_T = E_A = E_B$$
$$120 \text{ V} = 120 \text{ V} = 120 \text{ V}$$

We now have a parallel circuit with only two resistors, and they are of equal value. We have a choice of three different formulas that can be used to solve for the total resistance of the circuit.

(1) $\quad R_T = \dfrac{R_A \times R_B}{R_A + R_B} = \dfrac{60 \times 60}{60 + 60} = \dfrac{3600}{120} = 30 \text{ OHMS}$

(2) $\quad$ When the resistors of a parallel circuit are of equal value,

$\quad R_T = \dfrac{R}{N} = \dfrac{60}{2} = 30 \text{ OHMS} \qquad\qquad$ OR

(3) $\quad \dfrac{1}{R_T} = \dfrac{1}{R_A} + \dfrac{1}{R_B} = \dfrac{1}{60} + \dfrac{1}{60} = \dfrac{2}{60} = \dfrac{1}{30}$

$\quad \dfrac{1}{R_T} \rangle\!=\!\langle \dfrac{1}{30} \quad$ OR $\quad 1 \times R_T = 1 \times 30 \quad$ OR $\quad R_T = 30 \text{ OHMS}$

3. $\quad$ We know the values of E_T, R_T, E_A, R_A, E_B, R_B, R_1, R_2, R_3, and R_4.
Next we will solve for I_T, I_A, I_B, I_1, I_2, I_3, and I_4.

$\quad I_T \quad = \quad \dfrac{E_T}{R_T} \qquad$ OR $\quad \dfrac{120}{30} = 4 \qquad I_T = 4 \text{ AMPS}$

$\quad I_A \quad = \quad \dfrac{E_A}{R_A} \qquad$ OR $\quad \dfrac{120}{60} = 2 \qquad I_A = 2 \text{ AMPS}$

$\quad I_A \quad = \quad I_1 = I_2 \quad$ OR $\quad 2 = 2 = 2 \qquad I_1 = 2 \text{ AMPS}$

$\quad I_B \quad = \quad \dfrac{E_B}{R_B} = \qquad$ OR $\quad \dfrac{120}{60} = 2 \qquad I_B = 2 \text{ AMPS}$

$\quad I_B \quad = \quad I_3 = I_4 \quad$ OR $\quad 2 = 2 = 2 \qquad I_3 = 2 \text{ AMPS}$
$\qquad\qquad\qquad\qquad\qquad\qquad\qquad\qquad\qquad\qquad I_4 = 2 \text{ AMPS}$

(continued next page)

COMBINATION CIRCUITS

4. We know that resistors #1 and #2 of branch "A" are in series. We know too that resistors #3 and #4 of branch "B" are in series. We have determined that the total current of branch "A" is 2 AMPS, and the total current of branch "B" is 2 AMPS. By using the series formula, we can solve for the current of each branch.

BRANCH "A"
$$I_A = I_1 = I_2$$
$$2 = 2 = 2$$
$$I_1 = 2 \text{ AMPS}$$
$$I_2 = 2 \text{ AMPS}$$

BRANCH "B"
$$I_B = I_3 = I_4$$
$$2 = 2 = 2$$
$$I_3 = 2 \text{ AMPS}$$
$$I_4 = 2 \text{ AMPS}$$

5. We were given the resistance values of all resistors.
$R_1 = 20$ OHMS, $R_2 = 40$ OHMS, $R_3 = 10$ OHMS, and $R_4 = 50$ OHMS. By using OHM'S Law, we can determine the voltage drop across each resistor.

$$E_1 = R_1 \times I_1$$
$$= 20 \times 2$$
$$E_1 = 40 \text{ VOLTS}$$

$$E_3 = R_3 \times I_3$$
$$= 10 \times 2$$
$$E_3 = 20 \text{ VOLTS}$$

$$E_2 = R_2 \times I_2$$
$$= 40 \times 2$$
$$E_2 = 80 \text{ VOLTS}$$

$$E_4 = R_4 \times I_4$$
$$= 50 \times 2$$
$$E_4 = 100 \text{ VOLTS}$$

EXAMPLE 2: SERIES PARALLEL CIRCUIT.
Solve for all missing values.

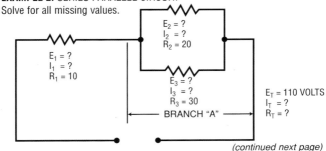

$E_2 = ?$
$I_2 = ?$
$R_2 = 20$

$E_1 = ?$
$I_1 = ?$
$R_1 = 10$

$E_3 = ?$
$I_3 = ?$
$R_3 = 30$

BRANCH "A"

$E_T = 110$ VOLTS
$I_T = ?$
$R_T = ?$

(continued next page)

COMBINATION CIRCUITS

To solve:

1.   We can see that resistors #2 and #3 are in parallel, and combined
     they are branch "A". When there are only two resistors, we use the
     following formula:

$$R_A = \frac{R_2 \times R_3}{R_2 + R_3} \quad OR \quad \frac{20 \times 30}{20 + 30} \quad OR \quad \frac{600}{50} \quad OR \quad 12 \; OHMS$$

2.   We can now re-draw our circuit as a simple series circuit.

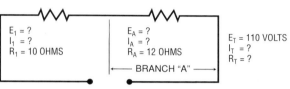

$E_1 = ?$
$I_1 = ?$
$R_1 = 10 \; OHMS$

$E_A = ?$
$I_A = ?$
$R_A = 12 \; OHMS$

$\longleftarrow$ BRANCH "A" $\longrightarrow$

$E_T = 110 \; VOLTS$
$I_T = ?$
$R_T = ?$

3.   In a series circuit,
     $R_T = R_1 + R_A$ OR $R_T = 10 + 12$ OR $22 \; OHMS$
     By using OHM'S Law,

$$I_T = \frac{E_T}{R_T} = \frac{110}{22} = 5 \; AMPS$$

In a series circuit,
$I_T = I_1 = I_A$ or $I_T = 5 \; AMPS$, $I_1 = 5 \; AMPS$, and $I_A = 5 \; AMPS$

By using OHM'S Law,
$E_1 = I_1 \times R_1 = 5 \times 10 = 50 \; VOLTS$
$E_T - E_1 = E_A$ or $110 - 50 = 60 \; VOLTS = E_A$

In a parallel circuit,
$E_A = E_2 = E_3$ or $E_A = 60 \; VOLTS$
$E_2 = 60 \; VOLTS$, and $E_3 = 60 \; VOLTS$

By using OHM'S Law,

$$I_2 = \frac{E_2}{R_2} = \frac{60}{20} = 3 \; AMPS$$

$$I_3 = \frac{E_3}{R_3} = \frac{60}{30} = 2 \; AMPS$$

(continued next page)

COMBINATION CIRCUITS

PROBLEM:

Solve for total resistance.

Re-draw circuit as many times as necessary.

Correct answer is 100 OHMS.

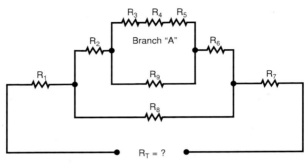

GIVEN VALUES:

R_1 = 15 OHMS	R_6 = 25 OHMS
R_2 = 35 OHMS	R_7 = 10 OHMS
R_3 = 50 OHMS	R_8 = 300 OHMS
R_4 = 40 OHMS	R_9 = 60 OHMS
R_5 = 30 OHMS	

COMMON ELECTRICAL DISTRIBUTION SYSTEMS

120/240 Volt Single Phase Three Wire System

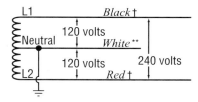

† • **Line one** ungrounded conductor colored **Black**.
† • **Line two** ungrounded conductor colored **Red**.
• Grounded neutral conductor colored **White or Gray.

120/240 Volt Three Phase Four Wire System (Delta High Leg)

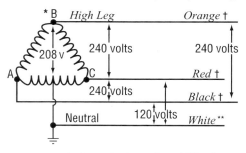

† • **A** phase ungrounded conductor colored **Black**.
†* • **B** phase ungrounded conductor colored **Orange** or tagged
   (High Leg). (Caution - 208V Orange to White)
† • **C** phase ungrounded conductor colored **Red**.
** • Grounded conductor colored **White** or Gray. (Center tap)

** Grounded conductors are required to be white or gray or three white stripes. See NEC 200.6A.
 * B phase of high leg delta must be Orange or tagged.
 † Ungrounded conductor colors may be other than shown; see local ordinances or specifications.

COMMON ELECTRICAL DISTRIBUTION SYSTEMS

120/208 Volt Three Phase Four Wire System (WYE Connected)

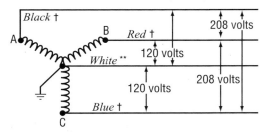

† • **A** phase ungrounded conductor colored **Black**.
† • **B** phase ungrounded conductor colored **Red**.
† • **C** phase ungrounded conductor colored **Blue**.
** • Grounded neutral conductor colored **White** or Gray.

277/480 Volt Three Phase Four Wire System (WYE Connected)

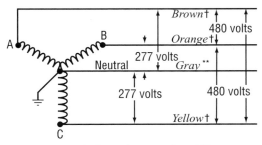

† • **A** phase ungrounded conductor colored **Brown**.
† • **B** phase ungrounded conductor colored **Purple**
† • **C** phase ungrounded conductor colored **Yellow**.
** • Grounded neutral conductor colored **Gray**.

** Grounded conductors are required to be white or gray or three white stripes. See NEC 200.6A.
  *B phase of high leg delta must be Orange or tagged.
  †Ungrounded conductor colors may be other than shown; see local ordinances or specifications.

ELECTRICAL FORMULAS FOR CALCULATING AMPERES, HORSEPOWER, KILOWATTS AND KVA

TO FIND	DIRECT CURRENT	ALTERNATING CURRENT		
		SINGLE PHASE	TWO PHASE-FOUR WIRE	THREE PHASE
AMPERES WHEN "HP" IS KNOWN	$\dfrac{HP \times 746}{E \times \%EFF}$	$\dfrac{HP \times 746}{E \times \%EFF \times PF}$	$\dfrac{HP \times 746}{E \times \%EFF \times PF \times 2}$	$\dfrac{HP \times 746}{E \times \%EFF \times PF \times 1.73}$
AMPERES WHEN "KW" IS KNOWN	$\dfrac{KW \times 1000}{E}$	$\dfrac{KW \times 1000}{E \times PF}$	$\dfrac{KW \times 1000}{E \times PF \times 2}$	$\dfrac{KW \times 1000}{E \times PF \times 1.73}$
AMPERES WHEN "KVA" IS KNOWN		$\dfrac{KVA \times 1000}{E}$	$\dfrac{KVA \times 1000}{E \times 2}$	$\dfrac{KVA \times 1000}{E \times 1.73}$
KILOWATTS (True Power)	$\dfrac{E \times I}{1000}$	$\dfrac{E \times I \times PF}{1000}$	$\dfrac{E \times I \times PF \times 2}{1000}$	$\dfrac{E \times I \times PF \times 1.73}{1000}$
KILOVOLT-AMPERES "KVA" (Apparent Power)		$\dfrac{E \times I}{1000}$	$\dfrac{E \times I \times 2}{1000}$	$\dfrac{E \times I \times 1.73}{1000}$
HORSEPOWER	$\dfrac{E \times I \times \%EFF}{746}$	$\dfrac{E \times I \times \%EFF \times PF}{746}$	$\dfrac{E \times I \times \%EFF \times PF \times 2}{746}$	$\dfrac{E \times I \times \%EFF \times PF \times 1.73}{746}$

PERCENT EFFICIENCY = % EFF = $\dfrac{\text{OUTPUT (WATTS)}}{\text{INPUT (WATTS)}}$ POWER FACTOR = PF = $\dfrac{\text{POWER USED (WATTS)}}{\text{APPARENT POWER}}$ = $\dfrac{KW}{KVA}$

E = VOLTS
I = AMPERES
W = WATTS

NOTE: DIRECT CURRENT FORMULAS DO NOT USE (PF, 2, OR 1.73)
SINGLE PHASE FORMULAS DO NOT USE (2 OR 1.73)
TWO PHASE - FOUR WIRE FORMULAS DO NOT USE (1.73)
THREE PHASE FORMULAS DO NOT USE (2)

TO FIND AMPERES

DIRECT CURRENT:

A.   When *HORSEPOWER* is known:

$$\text{AMPERES} = \frac{\text{HORSEPOWER x 746}}{\text{VOLTS x EFFICIENCY}} \quad \text{or} \quad I = \frac{\text{HP x 746}}{\text{E x \%EFF}}$$

What current will a travel-trailer toilet draw when equipped with a 12 volt, 1/8 HP motor, having a 96% efficiency rating?

$$I = \frac{\text{HP x 746}}{\text{E x \%EFF}} = \frac{746 \times 1/8}{12 \times 0.96} = \frac{93.25}{11.52} = 8.09 \text{ AMPS}$$

B.   When *KILOWATTS* are known:

$$\text{AMPERES} = \frac{\text{KILOWATTS x 1000}}{\text{VOLTS}} \quad \text{or} \quad I = \frac{\text{KW x 1000}}{\text{E}}$$

A 75 KW, 240 Volt, direct current generator is used to power a variable-speed conveyor belt at a rock crushing plant.
Determine the current.

$$I = \frac{\text{KW x 1000}}{\text{E}} = \frac{75 \times 1000}{240} = 312.5 \text{ AMPS}$$

SINGLE PHASE:

A.   When *WATTS, VOLTS, AND POWER FACTOR* are known:

$$\text{AMPERES} = \frac{\text{WATTS}}{\text{VOLTS x POWER FACTOR}} \quad \text{or} \quad \frac{\text{P}}{\text{E x PF}}$$

Determine the current when a circuit has a 1500 watt load, a power-factor of 86%, and operates from a single-phase 230 volt source.

$$I = \frac{1500}{230 \times 0.86} = \frac{1500}{197.8} = 7.58 \text{ AMPS}$$

TO FIND AMPERES

SINGLE PHASE:

B. When *HORSEPOWER* is known:

$$\text{AMPERES} = \frac{\text{HORSEPOWER x 746}}{\text{VOLTS x EFFICIENCY x POWER-FACTOR}}$$

Determine the amp-load of a single-phase, 1/2 HP, 115 volt motor.
The motor has an efficiency rating of 92%, and a power-factor of 80%.

$$I = \frac{HP \times 746}{E \times \%EFF \times PF} = \frac{1/2 \times 746}{115 \times 0.92 \times 0.80} = \frac{373}{84.64}$$

$$I = 4.4 \text{ AMPS}$$

C. When *KILOWATTS* are known:

$$\text{AMPERES} = \frac{\text{KILOWATTS x 1000}}{\text{VOLTS x POWER-FACTOR}} \quad \text{or} \quad I = \frac{KW \times 1000}{E \times PF}$$

A 230 Volt single-phase circuit has a 12KW power load, and operates
at 84% power-factor. Determine the current.

$$I = \frac{KW \times 1000}{E \times PF} = \frac{12 \times 1000}{230 \times 0.84} = \frac{12,000}{193.2} = 62 \text{ AMPS}$$

D. When *KILOVOLT-AMPERE* is known:

$$\text{AMPERES} = \frac{\text{KILOVOLT-AMPERE x 1000}}{\text{VOLTS}} \quad \text{or} \quad I = \frac{KVA \times 1000}{E}$$

A 115 volt, 2 KVA, single-phase generator operating at full load will
deliver 17.4 AMPERES. (Prove.)

$$I = \frac{2 \times 1000}{115} = \frac{2000}{115} = 17.4 \text{ AMPS}$$

REMEMBER:
    By definition, amperes is the rate of the flow of the current.

TO FIND AMPERES

THREE PHASE:

A. When _WATTS, VOLTS, AND POWER FACTOR are known_:

$$\text{AMPERES} = \frac{\text{WATTS}}{\text{VOLTS x POWER-FACTOR x 1.73}}$$

or

$$I = \frac{P}{E \text{ x } PF \text{ x } 1.73}$$

Determine the current when a circuit has a 1500 watt load, a power-factor of 86%, and operates from a three-phase, 230 volt source.

$$I = \frac{P}{E \text{ x } PF \text{ x } 1.73} = \frac{1500}{230 \text{ x } 0.86 \text{ x } 1.73} = \frac{1500}{342.2}$$

$$I = 4.4 \text{ AMPS}$$

B. When _HORSEPOWER_ is known:

$$\text{AMPERES} = \frac{\text{HORSEPOWER x 746}}{\text{VOLTS x EFFICIENCY x POWER-FACTOR x 1.73}}$$

or

$$I = \frac{HP \text{ x } 746}{E \text{ x } \%EFF \text{ x } PF \text{ x } 1.73}$$

Determine the amp-load of a three-phase, 1/2 HP, 230 volt motor. The motor has an efficiency rating of 92%, and a power-factor of 80%.

$$I = \frac{HP \text{ x } 746}{E \text{ x } \%EFF \text{ x } PF \text{ x } 1.73} = \frac{1/2 \text{ x } 746}{230 \text{ x } .92 \text{ x } .80 \text{ x } 1.73}$$

$$= \frac{373}{293} = 1.27 \text{ AMPS}$$

TO FIND AMPERES

THREE PHASE:

C. When *KILOWATTS are known*:

$$\text{AMPERES} = \frac{\text{KILOWATTS} \times 1000}{\text{VOLTS} \times \text{POWER-FACTOR} \times 1.73}$$

$$\text{or} \qquad I = \frac{\text{KW} \times 1000}{\text{E} \times \text{PF} \times 1.73}$$

A 230 volt, three-phase circuit, has a 12KW power load, and operates at 84% power-factor. Determine the current.

$$I = \frac{\text{KW} \times 1000}{\text{E} \times \text{PF} \times 1.73} = \frac{12,000}{230 \times 0.84 \times 1.73} = \frac{12,000}{334.24}$$

$I = 36$ AMPS

D. When *KILOVOLT-AMPERE* is known:

$$\text{AMPERES} = \frac{\text{KILOVOLT-AMPERE} \times 1000}{\text{E} \times 1.73} = \frac{\text{KVA} \times 1000}{\text{E} \times 1.73}$$

A 230 Volt, 4 KVA, three-phase generator operating at full load will deliver 10 AMPERES. (Prove.)

$$I = \frac{\text{KVA} \times 1000}{\text{E} \times 1.73} = \frac{4 \times 1000}{230 \times 1.73} = \frac{4000}{397.9}$$

$I = 10$ AMPS

NOTE: To better understand the preceding formulas:
  1. TWO-PHASE CURRENT x 2 = SINGLE-PHASE CURRENT.
  2. THREE-PHASE CURRENT x 1.73 = SINGLE-PHASE CURRENT
  3. THE CURRENT IN THE COMMON CONDUCTOR OF A TWO-PHASE (THREE WIRE) CIRCUIT IS 141% GREATER THAN EITHER OF THE OTHER TWO CONDUCTORS OF THAT CIRCUIT.

TO FIND HORSEPOWER

DIRECT CURRENT:

$$\text{HORSEPOWER} = \frac{\text{VOLTS x AMPERES x EFFICIENCY}}{746}$$

A 12 volt motor draws a current of 8.09 amperes, and has an efficiency rating of 96%. Determine the horsepower.

$$\text{HP} = \frac{\text{E x I x \%EFF}}{746} = \frac{12 \times 8.09 \times 0.96}{746} = \frac{93.19}{746}$$

$$\text{HP} = 0.1249 = 1/8 \text{ HP}$$

SINGLE-PHASE:

$$\text{HP} = \frac{\text{VOLTS x AMPERES x EFFICIENCY x POWER FACTOR}}{746}$$

A single-phase, 115 volt (AC) motor has an efficiency rating of 92%, and a power-factor of 80%. Determine the horsepower if the amp-load is 4.4 amperes.

$$\text{HP} = \frac{\text{E x I x \%EFF x PF}}{746} = \frac{115 \times 4.4 \times 0.92 \times 0.80}{746}$$

$$\text{HP} = \frac{372.416}{746} = 0.4992 = 1/2 \text{ HP}$$

THREE-PHASE:

$$\text{HP} = \frac{\text{VOLTS x AMPERES x EFFICIENCY x POWER FACTOR x 1.73}}{746}$$

A three-phase, 460 volt motor draws a current of 52 amperes. The motor has an efficiency rating of 94%, and a power factor of 80%. Determine the horsepower.

$$\text{HP} = \frac{\text{E x I x \%EFF x PF x 1.73}}{746} = \frac{460 \times 52 \times 0.94 \times 0.80 \times 1.73}{746}$$

$$\text{HP} = 41.7 \text{ HP}$$

TO FIND WATTS

The electrical power in any part of a circuit is equal to the current in that part multiplied by the voltage across that part of the circuit.

A watt is the power used when one volt causes one ampere to flow in a circuit.

One horsepower is the amount of energy required to lift 33,000 pounds, one foot, in one minute. The electrical equivalent of one horsepower is 745.6 watts. One watt is the amount of energy required to lift 44.26 pounds, one foot, in one minute. Watts is power, and power is the amount of work done in a given time.

When *VOLTS AND AMPERES* are known:

POWER (WATTS) = VOLTS x AMPERES

A 120 volt AC circuit draws a current of 5 amperes. Determine the power consumption.

P = E x I = 120 x 5 = 600 WATTS

We can now determine the resistance of this circuit.

POWER = RESISTANCE x (AMPERES)²

$P = R \times I^2$ or $600 = R \times 25$ *divide both sides of equation by 25*

$\dfrac{600}{25} = R$ or   R = 24 OHMS

or

$$\textbf{POWER} = \frac{\textbf{(VOLTS)}^2}{\textbf{RESISTANCE}} \quad \textbf{or} \quad P = \frac{E^2}{R} \quad \text{or} \quad 600 = \frac{120^2}{R}$$

$R \times 600 = 120^2$ or $R = \dfrac{14,400}{600} = 24$ OHMS

NOTE: REFER TO THE FORMULAS OF THE OHM'S LAW CHART ON PAGE 1

TO FIND KILOWATTS

DIRECT CURRENT:

$$\text{KILOWATTS} = \frac{\text{VOLTS x AMPERES}}{1000}$$

A 120 volt (DC) motor draws a current of 40 amperes.
Determine the kilowatts.

$$\text{KW} = \frac{\text{E x I}}{1000} = \frac{120 \times 40}{1000} = \frac{4800}{1000} = 4.8 \text{ KW}$$

SINGLE-PHASE:

$$\text{KILOWATTS} = \frac{\text{VOLTS x AMPERES x POWER FACTOR}}{1000}$$

A single-phase, 115 volt (AC) motor draws a current of 20 amperes,
and has a power-factor rating of 86%. Determine the kilowatts.

$$\text{KW} = \frac{\text{E x I x PF}}{1000} = \frac{115 \times 20 \times 0.86}{1000} = \frac{1978}{1000} = 1.978 = 2\text{KW}$$

THREE-PHASE:

$$\text{KILOWATTS} = \frac{\text{VOLTS x AMPERES x POWER FACTOR x 1.73}}{1000}$$

A three-phase, 460 volt (AC) motor draws a current of 52 amperes,
and has a power-factor rating of 80%. Determine the kilowatts.

$$\text{KW} = \frac{\text{E x I x PF x 1.73}}{1000} = \frac{460 \times 52 \times 0.80 \times 1.73}{1000}$$

$$= \frac{33,105}{1000} = 33.105 = 33\text{KW}$$

TO FIND KILOVOLT-AMPERES

SINGLE-PHASE:

KILOVOLT-AMPERES $= \dfrac{\text{VOLTS x AMPERES}}{1000}$

A single-phase, 240 volt generator delivers 41.66 amperes at full load. Determine the kilovolt-amperes rating.

KVA $= \dfrac{\text{E x I}}{1000} = \dfrac{240 \times 41.66}{1000} = \dfrac{10,000}{1000} = 10$ KVA

THREE-PHASE:

KILOVOLT-AMPERES $= \dfrac{\text{VOLTS x AMPERES x 1.73}}{1000}$

A three-phase, 460 volt generator delivers 52 amperes. Determine the kilovolt-amperes rating.

KVA $= \dfrac{\text{E x I x 1.73}}{1000} = \dfrac{460 \times 52 \times 1.73}{1000} = \dfrac{41,382}{1000}$

$= 41.382 = 41$ KVA

NOTE: KVA = APPARENT POWER = POWER BEFORE USED,
SUCH AS THE RATING OF A TRANSFORMER.

KIRCHHOFF'S LAWS

FIRST LAW (CURRENT):
THE SUM OF THE CURRENTS ARRIVING AT ANY POINT IN A CIRCUIT MUST EQUAL THE SUM OF THE CURRENTS LEAVING THAT POINT.
SECOND LAW (VOLTAGE):
THE TOTAL VOLTAGE APPLIED TO ANY CLOSED CIRCUIT PATH IS ALWAYS EQUAL TO THE SUM OF THE VOLTAGE DROPS IN THAT PATH.
OR
THE ALGEBRAIC SUM OF ALL THE VOLTAGES ENCOUNTERED IN ANY LOOP EQUALS ZERO.

TO FIND CAPACITANCE

CAPACITANCE (C):

$$C = \frac{Q}{E} \quad \text{or} \quad \text{CAPACITANCE} = \frac{\text{COULOMBS}}{\text{VOLTS}}$$

Capacitance is the property of a circuit or body that permits it to store an electrical charge equal to the accumulated charge divided by the voltage. Expressed in farads.

A. To determine the total capacity of capacitors, and/or condensers connected in series.

$$\frac{1}{C_T} = \frac{1}{C_1} + \frac{1}{C_2} + \frac{1}{C_3} + \frac{1}{C_4}$$

Determine the total capacity of four each, 12 microfarad capacitors connected in series.

$$\frac{1}{C_T} = \frac{1}{C_1} + \frac{1}{C_2} + \frac{1}{C_3} + \frac{1}{C_4}$$

$$= \frac{1}{12} + \frac{1}{12} + \frac{1}{12} + \frac{1}{12} = \frac{4}{12}$$

$$\frac{1}{C_T} = \frac{4}{12} \quad \text{or} \quad C_T \times 4 = 12 \quad \text{or} \quad C_T = \frac{12}{4} = 3 \text{ microfarads}$$

B. To determine the total capacity of capacitors, and/or condensers connected in parallel.

$$C_T = C_1 + C_2 + C_3 + C_4$$

Determine the total capacity of four each, 12 microfarad capacitors connected in parallel.

$$C_T = C_1 + C_2 + C_3 + C_4$$

$$C_T = 12 + 12 + 12 + 12 = 48 \text{ microfarads}$$

A farad is the unit of capacitance of a condenser that retains one coulomb of charge with one volt difference of potential.
1 Farad = 1,000,000 Microfarads

6-DOT COLOR CODE FOR MICA AND MOLDED PAPER CAPACITORS

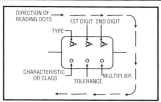

TYPE	COLOR	1ST DIGIT	2ND DIGIT	MULTIPLIER	TOLERANCE (%)	CHARACTERISTIC OR CLASS
JAN, MICA	BLACK	0	0	1	± 1	
	BROWN	1	1	10	± 2	
	RED	2	2	100	± 3	
	ORANGE	3	3	1,000	± 4	
	YELLOW	4	4	10,000	± 5	APPLIES TO
	GREEN	5	5	100,000	± 6	TEMPERATURE
	BLUE	6	6	1,000,000	± 7	COEFFICIENT
	VIOLET	7	7	10,000,000	± 8	OR METHODS
	GRAY	8	8	100,000,000	± 9	OF TESTING
ETA, MICA	WHITE	9	9	1,000,000,000		
	GOLD			.1	± 10	
MOLDED PAPER	SILVER			.01	± 20	
	BODY					

RESISTOR COLOR CODE

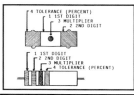

COLOR	1ST DIGIT	2ND DIGIT	MULTIPLIER	TOLERANCE (%)
BLACK	0	0	1	
BROWN	1	1	10	
RED	2	2	100	
ORANGE	3	3	1,000	
YELLOW	4	4	10,000	
GREEN	5	5	100,000	
BLUE	6	6	1,000,000	
VIOLET	7	7	10,000,000	
GRAY	8	8	100,000,000	
WHITE	9	9	1,000,000,000	
GOLD			.1	± 5%
SILVER			.01	± 10%
NO COLOR				± 20%

MAXIMUM PERMISSIBLE CAPACITOR KVAR FOR USE WITH
OPEN-TYPE THREE-PHASE SIXTY-CYCLE INDUCTION MOTORS

MOTOR RATING HP	3600 RPM		1800 RPM		1200 RPM	
	MAXIMUM CAPACITOR RATING KVAR	REDUCTION IN LINE CURRENT %	MAXIMUM CAPACITOR RATING KVAR	REDUCTION IN LINE CURRENT %	MAXIMUM CAPACITOR RATING KVAR	REDUCTION IN LINE CURRENT %
10	3	10	3	11	3.5	14
15	4	9	4	10	5	13
20	5	9	5	10	6.5	12
25	6	9	6	10	7.5	11
30	7	8	7	9	9	11
40	9	8	9	9	11	10
50	12	8	11	9	13	10
60	14	8	14	8	15	10
75	17	8	16	8	18	10
100	22	8	21	8	25	9
125	27	8	26	8	30	9
150	32.5	8	30	8	35	9
200	40	8	37.5	8	42.5	9

MOTOR RATING HP	900 RPM		720 RPM		600 RPM	
	MAXIMUM CAPACITOR RATING KVAR	REDUCTION IN LINE CURRENT %	MAXIMUM CAPACITOR RATING KVAR	REDUCTION IN LINE CURRENT %	MAXIMUM CAPACITOR RATING KVAR	REDUCTION IN LINE CURRENT %
10	5	21	6.5	27	7.5	31
15	6.5	18	8	23	9.5	27
20	7.5	16	9	21	12	25
25	9	15	11	20	14	23
30	10	14	12	18	16	22
40	12	13	15	16	20	20
50	15	12	19	15	24	19
60	18	11	22	15	27	19
75	21	10	26	14	32.5	18
100	27	10	32.5	13	40	17
125	32.5	10	40	13	47.5	16
150	37.5	10	47.5	12	52.5	15
200	47.5	10	60	12	65	14

NOTE: If capacitors of a lower rating than the values given in the table are used, the percentage reduction in line current given in the table should be reduced proportionately.

POWER-FACTOR CORRECTION

TABLE VALUES x KW OF CAPACITORS NEEDED TO CORRECT
FROM EXISTING TO DESIRED POWER FACTOR

EXISTING POWER FACTOR %	CORRECTED POWER FACTOR					
	100%	95%	90%	85%	80%	75%
50	1.732	1.403	1.247	1.112	0.982	0.850
52	1.643	1.314	1.158	1.023	0.893	0.761
54	1.558	1.229	1.073	0.938	0.808	0.676
55	1.518	1.189	1.033	0.898	0.768	0.636
56	1.479	1.150	0.994	0.859	0.729	0.597
58	1.404	1.075	0.919	0.784	0.654	0.522
60	1.333	1.004	0.848	0.713	0.583	0.451
62	1.265	0.936	0.780	0.645	0.515	0.383
64	1.201	0.872	0.716	0.581	0.451	0.319
65	1.168	0.839	0.683	0.548	0.418	0.286
66	1.139	0.810	0.654	0.519	0.389	0.257
68	1.078	0.749	0.593	0.458	0.328	0.196
70	1.020	0.691	0.535	0.400	0.270	0.138
72	0.964	0.635	0.479	0.344	0.214	0.082
74	0.909	0.580	0.424	0.289	0.159	0.027
75	0.882	0.553	0.397	0.262	0.132	
76	0.855	0.526	0.370	0.235	0.105	
78	0.802	0.473	0.317	0.182	0.052	
80	0.750	0.421	0.265	0.130		
82	0.698	0.369	0.213	0.078		
84	0.646	0.317	0.161			
85	0.620	0.291	0.135			
86	0.594	0.265	0.109			
88	0.540	0.211	0.055			
90	0.485	0.156				
92	0.426	0.097				
94	0.363	0.034				
95	0.329					

TYPICAL PROBLEM: With a load of 500 KW at 70% power factor, it is desired to find the KVA of capacitors required to correct the power factor to 85%

SOLUTION: From the table, select the multiplying factor 0.400 corresponding to the existing 70%, and the corrected 85% power factor.
0.400 x 500 = 200 KVA of capacitors required.

POWER FACTOR AND EFFICIENCY EXAMPLE

A squirrel cage induction motor is rated 10 horsepower, 208 volt, three phase and has a nameplate rating of 27.79 amperes. A wattmeter reading indicates 8 kilowatts of consumed (true) power. Calculate apparent power (KVA), power factor, efficiency, internal losses and size the capacitor in kilo-volts reactive (KVAR) needed to correct the power factor to unity (100%).

Apparent input power: kilovolt-amperes (KVA)
KVA = (E x I x 1.73) / 1000 = (208 x 27.79 x 1.73) / 1000 = **10 KVA**

Power factor (PF) = ratio of true power (KW) to apparent power (KVA).
Kilo-watts / kilo-volt-amperes = 8KW/10 KVA = .8 = **80% Power Factor**
80% of the 10-KVA apparent power input performs work.

Motor output in kilowatts = 10 horsepower x 746 watts = 7460 watts = **7.46 KW.**
Efficiency = watts out/watts in = 7.46 KW / 8KW = .9325 = **93.25% Efficiency.**

Internal losses (heat, friction, hysteresis) = 8KW - 7.46 KW = **.54 KW** (540 watts)

Kilovolt-amperes reactive (KVAR)   (Power stored in motor magnetic field)
KVAR = $\sqrt{KVA^2 - KW^2}$ = $\sqrt{10KVA^2 - 8KW^2}$ = $\sqrt{100-64}$ = $\sqrt{36}$ = **6 KVAR**
The size capacitor needed to equal the motor's stored reactive power is 6 KVAR. (A capacitor stores reactive power in its electrostatic field).

The power source must supply the current to perform work and maintain the motor's magnetic field. Before power factor correction, this was 27.79 amperes. The motor magnetizing current after power factor correction is supplied by circulation of current between the motor and the electrostatic field of the capacitor and is no longer supplied by power source after initial start up.
The motor feeder current after correction to 100% will equal the amount required by the input watts in this case (8 KW x 1000) / (208 volts x 1.73) = **22.23 amps**

• kilo = 1000   example: 1000 watts = 1 kilowatt
• inductive loads (motors, coils) have lagging currents and capacitive loads have
  leading currents.
• inductance and capacitance have opposite effects in a circuit and can cancel each other

TO FIND INDUCTANCE

INDUCTANCE (L):

Inductance is the production of magnetization of electrification in a body by the proximity of a magnetic field or electric charge, or of the electric current in a conductor by the variation of the magnetic field in its vicinity. Expressed in Henrys.

A. To find the total inductance of coils connected in series.

$L_T = L_1 + L_2 + L_3 + L_4$

Determine the total inductance of four coils connected in series. Each coil has an inductance of four Henrys.

$L_T = L_1 + L_2 + L_3 + L_4$

$= 4 + 4 + 4 + 4 = 16$ Henrys

B. To find the total inductance of coils connected in parallel.

$$\frac{1}{L_T} = \frac{1}{L_1} + \frac{1}{L_2} + \frac{1}{L_3} + \frac{1}{L_4}$$

Determine the total inductance of four coils connected in parallel. Each coil has an inductance of four Henrys.

$$\frac{1}{L_T} = \frac{1}{L_1} + \frac{1}{L_2} + \frac{1}{L_3} + \frac{1}{L_4}$$

$$\frac{1}{L_T} = \frac{1}{4} + \frac{1}{4} + \frac{1}{4} + \frac{1}{4}$$

$$\frac{1}{L_T} = \frac{4}{4} \quad \text{OR} \quad L_T \times 4 = 1 \times 4 \quad \text{OR} \quad L_T = \frac{4}{4} = 1 \text{ Henry}$$

An induction coil is a device, consisting of two concentric coils and an interrupter, that changes a low steady voltage into a high intermittent alternating voltage by electromagnetic induction. Most often used as a spark coil.

TO FIND IMPEDANCE

IMPEDANCE (Z):

Impedance is the total opposition to an alternating current presented by a circuit. Expressed in OHMS.

A. When *VOLTS AND AMPERES* are known:

$$\text{IMPEDANCE} = \frac{\text{VOLTS}}{\text{AMPERES}} \quad \text{OR} \quad Z = \frac{E}{I}$$

Determine the impedance of a 120 volt A-C circuit that draws a current of four amperes.

$$Z = \frac{E}{I} = \frac{120}{4} = 30 \text{ OHMS}$$

B. When *RESISTANCE AND REACTANCE* are known:

$$Z = \sqrt{\text{RESISTANCE}^2 + \text{REACTANCE}^2} = \sqrt{R^2 + X^2}$$

Determine the impedance of an A-C circuit when the resistance is 6 OHMS, and the reactance is 8 OHMS.

$$Z = \sqrt{R^2 + X^2} = \sqrt{36 + 64} = \sqrt{100} = 10 \text{ OHMS}$$

C. When *RESISTANCE, INDUCTIVE REACTANCE, AND CAPACITIVE REACTANCE* are known:

$$Z = \sqrt{R^2 + (X_L - X_C)^2}$$

Determine the impedance of an A-C circuit which has a resistance of 6 OHMS, an inductive reactance of 18 OHMS, and a capacitive reactance of 10 OHMS.

$$Z = \sqrt{R^2 + (X_L - X_C)^2}$$
$$= \sqrt{6^2 + (18 - 10)^2} = \sqrt{6^2 + (8)^2}$$
$$= \sqrt{36 + 64} = \sqrt{100} = 10 \text{ OHMS}$$

TO FIND REACTANCE

REACTANCE (X):

Reactance in a circuit is the opposition to an alternating current caused by inductance and capacitance, equal to the difference between capacitive and inductive reactance. Expressed in OHMS.

A. INDUCTIVE REACTANCE X_L

Inductive reactance is that element of reactance in a circuit caused by self-inductance.

$$X_L = 2 \times 3.1416 \times \textbf{FREQUENCY} \times \textbf{INDUCTANCE}$$
$$= 6.28 \times F \times L$$

Determine the reactance of a four-Henry coil on a 60 cycle, A-C circuit.

$$X_L = 6.28 \times F \times L = 6.28 \times 60 \times 4 = 1507 \text{ OHMS}$$

B. CAPACITIVE REACTANCE X_C

Capacitive reactance is that element of reactance in a circuit caused by capacitance.

$$X_C = \frac{1}{2 \times 3.1416 \times \textbf{FREQUENCY} \times \textbf{CAPACITANCE}}$$

$$= \frac{1}{6.28 \times F \times C}$$

Determine the reactance of a four microfarad condenser on a 60 cycle, A-C circuit.

$$X_C = \frac{1}{6.28 \times F \times C} = \frac{1}{6.28 \times 60 \times .000004}$$

$$= \frac{1}{0.0015072} = 663 \text{ OHMS}$$

A HENRY is a unit of inductance, equal to the inductance of a circuit in which the variation of a current at the rate of one ampere per second induces an electromotive force of one volt.

FULL-LOAD CURRENT IN AMPERES
DIRECT CURRENT MOTORS

HP	Armature Voltage Rating*					
	90V	120V	180V	240V	500V	550V
1/4	4.0	3.1	2.0	1.6	–	–
1/3	5.2	4.1	2.6	2.0	–	–
1/2	6.8	5.4	3.4	2.7	–	–
3/4	9.6	7.6	4.8	3.8	–	–
1	12.2	9.5	6.1	4.7	–	–
1-1/2	–	13.2	8.3	6.6	–	–
2	–	17	10.8	8.5	–	–
3	–	25	16	12.2	–	–
5	–	40	27	20	–	–
7-1/2	–	58	–	29	13.6	12.2
10	–	76	–	38	18	16
15	–	–	–	55	27	24
20	–	–	–	72	34	31
25	–	–	–	89	43	38
30	–	–	–	106	51	46
40	–	–	–	140	67	61
50	–	–	–	173	83	75
60	–	–	–	206	99	90
75	–	–	–	255	123	111
100	–	–	–	341	164	148
125	–	–	–	425	205	185
150	–	–	–	506	246	222
200	–	–	–	675	330	294

These values of full-load currents* are for motors running at base speed.

* These are average dc quantities.

Reprinted with permission from NFPA 70-2008, the *National Electrical Code*®, Copyright 2007, National Fire Protection Association, Quincy, MA 02269. This reprinted material is not the referenced subject which is represented only by the Standard in its entirety.

DIRECT CURRENT MOTORS

TERMINAL MARKINGS:

Terminal markings are used to tag terminals to which connections are to be made from outside circuits.

Facing the end opposite the drive (commutator end) the standard direction of shaft rotation is counter-clockwise.

A-1 and A-2 indicate armature leads.
S-1 and S-2 indicate series-field leads.
F-1 and F-2 indicate shunt-field leads.

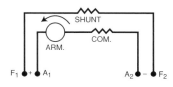

SHUNT WOUND MOTORS

To change rotation, reverse either armature leads or shunt leads. <u>Do not</u> reverse both armature and shunt leads.

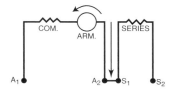

SERIES WOUND MOTORS

To change rotation, reverse either armature leads or series leads. <u>Do not</u> reverse both armature and series leads.

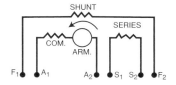

COMPOUND WOUND MOTORS

To change rotation, reverse either armature leads or both the series and shunt leads. <u>Do not</u> reverse all three sets of leads.

Note: Standard rotation for <u>D.C. Generator</u> is clockwise.

FULL-LOAD CURRENT IN AMPERES
SINGLE-PHASE ALTERNATING CURRENT MOTORS

HP	115V	200V	208V	230V
1/6	4.4	2.5	2.4	2.2
1/4	5.8	3.3	3.2	2.9
1/3	7.2	4.1	4.0	3.6
1/2	9.8	5.6	5.4	4.9
3/4	13.8	7.9	7.6	6.9
1	16	9.2	8.8	8.0
1-1/2	20	11.5	11	10
2	24	13.8	13.2	12
3	34	19.6	18.7	17
5	56	32.2	30.8	28
7-1/2	80	46	44	40
10	100	57.5	55	50

The voltages listed are rated motor voltages. The listed currents are for system voltage ranges of 110 to 120 and 220 to 240.

SINGLE-PHASE USING STANDARD THREE-PHASE STARTER

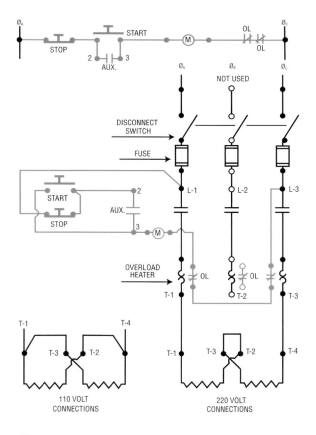

110 VOLT CONNECTIONS

220 VOLT CONNECTIONS

Ⓜ = MOTOR STARTER COIL

SINGLE PHASE MOTORS

SPLIT-PHASE----SQUIRREL CAGE----DUAL-VOLTAGE

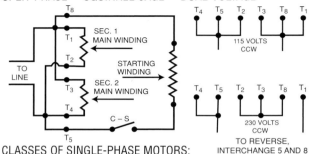

CLASSES OF SINGLE-PHASE MOTORS:

1. SPLIT-PHASE
   A. CAPACITOR-START
   B. REPULSION-START
   C. RESISTANCE-START
   D. SPLIT-CAPACITOR

2. COMMUTATOR
   A. REPULSION
   B. SERIES

TERMINAL COLOR MARKING:

T_1 <u>BLUE</u>	T_3 <u>ORANGE</u>	T_5 <u>BLACK</u>
T_2 <u>WHITE</u>	T_4 <u>YELLOW</u>	T_8 <u>RED</u>

NOTE: Split-phase motors are usually fractional horsepower. The majority of electric motors used in washing machines, refrigerators, etc. are of the split-phase type.

To change the speed of a split-phase motor, the number of poles must be changed.

1. Addition of running winding
2. Two starting windings, and two running windings
3. Consequent pole connections

SINGLE PHASE MOTORS

SPLIT-PHASE----SQUIRREL CAGE
A. RESISTANCE START:

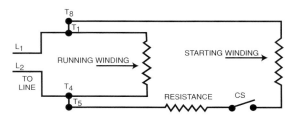

Centrifugal switch (CS) opens after reaching 75% of normal speed.

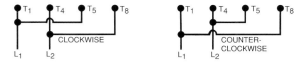

B. CAPACITOR START:

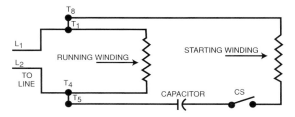

Note: 1. A resistance start motor has a resistance connected in
series with the starting winding.
2. The capacitor start motor is employed where a high
starting torque is required.

RUNNING OVERLOAD UNITS

KIND OF MOTOR	SUPPLY SYSTEM	NUMBER & LOCATION OF OVER-LOAD UNITS, SUCH AS TRIP COILS OR RELAYS
1-Phase ac or dc	2-wire, 1-phase ac or dc, ungrounded	1 in either conductor
1-Phase ac or dc	2-wire, 1-phase ac or dc, one conductor ungrounded	1 in ungrounded conductor
1-Phase ac or dc	3-wire, 1-phase ac or dc, grounded neutral conductor	1 in either ungrounded conductor
1-Phase ac	any 3-phase	1 in ungrounded conductor
2-Phase ac	3-wire, 2-phase ac, ungrounded	2, one in each phase
2-Phase ac	3-wire, 2-phase ac, one conductor grounded	2 in ungrounded conductors
2-Phase ac	4-wire, 2-phase ac, grounded or ungrounded	2, one per phase in ungrounded conductors
2-Phase ac	5-wire, 2-phase ac, grounded neutral or ungrounded	2, one per phase in any ungrounded phase wire
3-Phase ac	any 3-phase	3, one in each phase*

* Exception: Where protected by other approved means.

MOTOR BRANCH - CIRCUIT PROTECTIVE DEVICES
MAXIMUM RATING OR SETTING

	Percent of Full-Load Current			
Type of Motor	Nontime Delay Fuse*	Dual Element (Time-Delay) Fuse*	Instantaneous Trip Breaker	Inverse Time Breaker**
Single-phase motors	300	175	800	250
AC polyphase motors other than wound-rotor Squirrel Cage:	300	175	800	250
Other than Design B Energy Efficient	300	175	800	250
Design B Energy Efficient	300	175	1100	250
Synchronous***	300	175	800	250
Wound rotor	150	150	800	150
Direct-current (constant voltage)	150	150	250	150

For certain exceptions to the values specified, see Sections 430-52 – 430-54.
*   The values in the Nontime Delay Fuse column apply to Time-Delay Class CC fuses.
** The values given in the last column also cover the ratings of nonadjustable inverse time types of circuit breakers that may be modified as in Section 430-52.
*** Synchronous motors of the low-torque, low speed type (usually 450 rpm or lower), such as are used to drive reciprocating compressors, pumps, etc., that start unloaded, do not require a fuse rating or circuit-breaker setting in excess of 200% of full-load current.

FULL-LOAD CURRENT
THREE-PHASE ALTERNATING CURRENT MOTORS

HP	Induction Type Squirrel-Cage and Wound-Rotor Amperes							Synchronous Type Unity Power Factor* Amperes			
	115 Volts	200 Volts	208 Volts	230 Volts	460 Volts	575 Volts	2300 Volts	230 Volts	460 Volts	575 Volts	2300 Volts
$\frac{1}{2}$	4.4	2.5	2.4	2.2	1.1	0.9	-	-	-	-	-
$\frac{3}{4}$	6.4	3.7	3.5	3.2	1.6	1.3	-	-	-	-	-
1	8.4	4.8	4.6	4.2	2.1	1.7	-	-	-	-	-
$1\frac{1}{2}$	12.0	6.9	6.6	6.0	3.0	2.4	-	-	-	-	-
2	13.6	7.8	7.5	6.8	3.4	2.7	-	-	-	-	-
3	-	11.0	10.6	9.6	4.8	3.9	-	-	-	-	-
5	-	17.5	16.7	15.2	7.6	6.1	-	-	-	-	-
$7\frac{1}{2}$	-	25.3	24.2	22	11	9	-	-	-	-	-
10	-	32.2	30.8	28	14	11	-	-	-	-	-
15	-	48.3	46.2	42	21	17	-	-	-	-	-
20	-	62.1	59.4	54	27	22	-	-	-	-	-
25	-	78.2	74.8	68	34	27	-	53	26	21	-
30	-	92	88	80	40	32	-	63	32	26	-
40	-	120	114	104	52	41	-	83	41	33	-
50	-	150	143	130	65	52	-	104	52	42	-
60	-	177	169	154	77	62	16	123	61	49	12
75	-	221	211	192	96	77	20	155	78	62	15
100	-	285	273	248	124	99	26	202	101	81	20
125	-	359	343	312	156	125	31	253	126	101	25
150	-	414	396	360	180	144	37	302	151	121	30
200	-	552	528	480	240	192	49	400	201	161	40
250	-	-	-	-	302	242	60	-	-	-	-
300	-	-	-	-	361	289	72	-	-	-	-
350	-	-	-	-	414	336	83	-	-	-	-
400	-	-	-	-	477	382	95	-	-	-	-
450	-	-	-	-	515	412	103	-	-	-	-
500	-	-	-	-	590	472	118	-	-	-	-

The voltages listed are rated motor voltages. The currents listed shall be permitted for system voltage ranges of 110 to 120, 220 to 240, 440 to 480, and 550-600 volts.
* For 90 and 80 percent power factor, the above figures shall be multiplied by 1.1 and 1.25 respectively.

Reprinted with permission from NFPA 70-2008, the *National Electrical Code*®, Copyright 2007, National Fire Protection Association, Quincy, MA 02269. This reprinted material is not the referenced subject which is represented only by the Standard in its entirety.

FULL-LOAD CURRENT AND OTHER DATA
THREE PHASE A.C. MOTORS

MOTOR HORSEPOWER		MOTOR AMPERE	SIZE BREAKER	SIZE STARTER	HEATER AMPERE **	SIZE WIRE	SIZE CONDUIT
¹/₂	230V	2.2	15	00	2.530	12	³/₄"
	460	1.1	15	00	1.265	12	³/₄
³/₄	230	3.2	15	00	3.680	12	³/₄
	460	1.6	15	00	1.840	12	³/₄
1	230	4.2	15	00	4.830	12	³/₄
	460	2.1	15	00	2.415	12	³/₄
1¹/₂	230	6.0	15	00	6.900	12	³/₄
	460	3.0	15	00	3.450	12	³/₄
2	230	6.8	15	0	7.820	12	³/₄
	460	3.4	15	00	3.910	12	³/₄
3	230	9.6	20	0	11.040	12	³/₄
	460	4.8	15	0	5.520	12	³/₄
5	230	15.2	30	1	17.480	12	³/₄
	460	7.6	15	0	8.740	12	³/₄
7¹/₂	230	22	45	1	25.300	10	³/₄
	460	11	20	1	12.650	12	³/₄
10	230	28	60	2	32.200	10	³/₄
	460	14	30	1	16.100	12	³/₄
15	230	42	70	2	48.300	6	1
	460	21	40	2	24.150	10	³/₄
20	230	54	100	3	62.100	4	1
	460	27	50	2	31.050	10	³/₄
25	230	68	100	3	78.200	4	1¹/₂
	460	34	50	2	39.100	8	1
30	230	80	125	3	92.000	3	1¹/₂
	460	40	70	3	46.000	8	1
40	230	104	175	4	119.600	1	1¹/₂
	460	52	100	3	59.800	6	1
50	230	130	200	4	149.500	00	2
	460	65	150	3	74.750	4	1¹/₂

*   Overcurrent device may have to be increased due to starting current and load conditions.
    See NEC 430-52, Table 430-52. Wire size based on 75°C terminations and 75°C insulation.
** Overload heater must be based on motor nameplate & sized per NEC 430-32.
*** Conduit size based on Rigid Metal Conduit with some spare capacity. For minimum size &
other conduit types, see NEC Appendix C, or *UGLY'S pages 83 - 103.*

FULL-LOAD CURRENT AND OTHER DATA
THREE PHASE A.C. MOTORS

MOTOR HORSEPOWER		MOTOR AMPERE	SIZE BREAKER	SIZE STARTER	HEATER AMPERE **	SIZE WIRE	SIZE CONDUIT
60	230V	154	250	5	177.10	000	2"
	460	77	200	4	88.55	3	1¹/₂
75	230	192	300	5	220.80	250kcmil	2¹/₂
	460	96	200	4	110.40	1	1¹/₂
100	230	248	400	5	285.20	350kcmil	3
	460	124	200	4	142.60	2/0	2
125	230	312	500	6	358.80	600kcmil	3¹/₂
	460	156	250	5	179.40	000	2
150	230	360	600	6	414.00	700kcmil	4
	460	180	300	5	207.00	0000	2¹/₂

MOTOR AND MOTOR CIRCUIT CONDUCTOR PROTECTION

Motors can have large starting currents three to five times or more than that of the actual motor current. In order for motors to start, the motor and motor circuit conductors are allowed to be protected by circuit breakers and fuses at values that are higher than the actual motor and conductor ampere ratings. These larger overcurrent devices do not provide overload protection and will only open upon short circuits or ground faults. Overload protection must be used to protect the motor based on the actual nameplate amperes of the motor. This protection is usually in the form of heating elements in manual or magnetic motor starters. Small motors such as waste disposal motors have a red overload reset button built into the motor.

GENERAL MOTOR RULES

- Use Full Load Current from Tables instead of nameplate.
- Branch Circuit Conductors - Use 125% of Full Load Current to find conductor size.
- Branch Circuit OCP Size - Use percentages given in Tables for Full Load Current. (UGLY'S page 35)
- Feeder Conductor Size - 125% of largest motor and sum of the rest.
- Feeder OCP - Use largest OCP plus rest of Full Load Currents
- See examples UGLY'S page 42

MOTOR BRANCH CIRCUIT AND FEEDER EXAMPLE
GENERAL MOTOR APPLICATIONS

Branch Circuit Conductors: Use Full Load Three Phase Currents;
From Table UGLY'S Page 39 or 2005 NEC Table 430.250,
50 HP 480 volt three phase motor design B, 75 degree terminations
= 65 Amperes
125% of Full Load Current (NEC 430.22(A) (UGLY'S page 41)
125% of 65 A = **81.25 Amperes** Conductor Selection Ampacity

Branch Circuit Over Current Device: NEC 430.52 (C1)
(Branch Circuit Short Circuit and Ground Fault Protection)
Use percentages given in UGLY'S Page 35 or 2005 NEC 430.52 for
Type of circuit breaker or fuse used.
50 HP 480 V 3 Ph Motor = 65 Amperes from UGLY'S Page 39.
Nontime Fuse = 300% from UGLY'S Page 35.
300% of 65A = 195 A. NEC 430.52(C1)(EX1) Next size allowed
NEC 240.6A = **200 Ampere Fuse**.

Feeder Connectors: For 50 HP and 30 HP 480 Volt Three phase
design B motors on same feeder
Use 125% of largest full load current and 100% of rest. (NEC 430.24)
50 HP 480 V 3 Ph Motor = 65A; 30 HP 480 V 3 Ph Motor = 40A
(125% of 65A) + 40A = **121.25 A** Conductor Selection Ampacity

Feeder Overcurrent Device: (NEC 430.62(A)
(Feeder short circuit and ground fault protection)
Use largest over current protection device <u>plus</u> full load currents of
the rest of the motors.
50 HP = 200 A fuse   (65 FLC)
30 HP = 125 A fuse   (40 FLC)
200 A fuse + 40 A (FLC) = 240 A. Do not exceed this value on
feeder. Go down to a **225 A** fuse.

LOCKED ROTOR CODE LETTERS

Code Letter	Kilovolt-Ampere per Horsepower with Locked Rotor	Code Letter	Kilovolt-Ampere per Horsepower with Locked Rotor
A	0 - 3.14	L	9.0 - 9.99
B	3.15 - 3.54	M	10.0 - 11.19
C	3.55 - 3.99	N	11.2 - 12.49
D	4.0 - 4.49	P	12.5 - 13.99
E	4.5 - 4.99	R	14.0 - 15.99
F	5.0 - 5.59	S	16.0 - 17.99
G	5.6 - 6.29	T	18.0 - 19.99
H	6.3 - 7.09	U	20.0 - 22.39
J	7.1 - 7.99	V	22.4 and up
K	8.0 - 8.99		

The National Electrical Code® requires that all alternating current motors rated 1/2 horsepower or more (except for polyphase wound rotor motors) must have code letters on their nameplates indicating motor input with locked rotor (in kilovolt-amperes per horsepower). If you know the horsepower and voltage rating of a motor and its "Locked KVA per Horsepower" (from above table), you can calculate the locked rotor current using the following formulas.

Single Phase Motors:

$$\text{Locked Rotor Current} = \frac{HP \times KVA_{hp} \times 1000}{E}$$

Three Phase Motors:

$$\text{Locked Rotor Current} = \frac{HP \times KVA_{hp} \times 1000}{E \times 1.73}$$

Example: What is the maximum locked rotor current for a 480 volt 25 horsepower code letter F motor?

(from the above table, code letter F = 5.59 KVA$_{hp}$)

$$I = \frac{HP \times KVA_{hp} \times 1000}{E \times 1.73} = \frac{25 \times 5.59 \times 1000}{480 \times 1.73} = \textbf{168.29 Amperes}$$

Reprinted with permission from NFPA 70-2008, the *National Electrical Code* ®, Copyright 2007, National Fire Protection Association, Quincy, MA 02269. This reprinted material is not the referenced subject which is represented only by the Standard in its entirety.

MAXIMUM MOTOR LOCKED ROTOR CURRENT

HP	115V	208V	230V	HP	115V	208V	230V
1/2	58.8	32.5	29.4	3	204	113	102
3/4	82.8	45.8	41.4	5	336	186	168
1	96	53	48	7-1/2	480	265	240
1-1/2	120	66	60	10	600	332	300
2	144	80	72				

MAXIMUM MOTOR LOCKED ROTOR CURRENT
in AMPERES, TWO & THREE PHASE, DESIGN B, C AND D **

HP	115V	200V	208V	230V	460V	575V
1/2	40	23	22.1	20	10	8
3/4	50	28.8	27.6	25	12.5	10
1	60	34.5	33	30	15	12
1-1/2	80	46	44	40	20	16
2	100	57.5	55	50	25	20
3	–	73.6	71	64	32	25.6
5	–	105.8	102	92	46	36.8
7-1/2	–	146	140	127	63.5	50.8
10	–	186.3	179	162	81	64.8
15	–	267	257	232	116	93
20	–	334	321	290	145	116
25	–	420	404	365	183	146
30	–	500	481	435	218	174
40	–	667	641	580	290	232
50	–	834	802	725	363	290
60	–	1001	962	870	435	348
75	–	1248	1200	1085	543	434
100	–	1668	1603	1450	725	580
125	–	2087	2007	1815	908	726
150	–	2496	2400	2170	1085	868
200	–	3335	3207	2900	1450	1160

* Conversion Table for Selection of Disconnecting Means and Controllers as Determined from Horsepower and Voltage Rating. For use only with 430.110, 440.12, 440.41 and 455.8(C).

** Conversion Table for Selection of Disconnecting Means and Controllers as Determined from Horsepower and Voltage Rating and Design Letter. For use only with 430.110, 440.12, 440.41 and 455.8(C).

THREE PHASE A.C. MOTOR WINDINGS AND CONNECTIONS

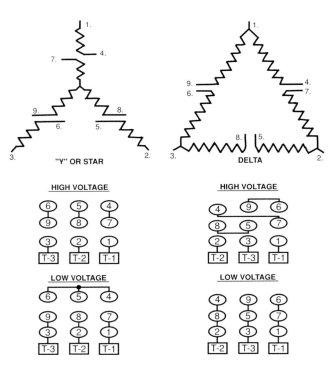

"Y" OR STAR

DELTA

HIGH VOLTAGE

HIGH VOLTAGE

LOW VOLTAGE

LOW VOLTAGE

Note: 1. The most important part of any motor is the name plate. Check the data given on the plate before making the connections.

2. To change rotation direction of 3 phase motor, swap any 2 T-leads.

THREE WIRE STOP-START STATION

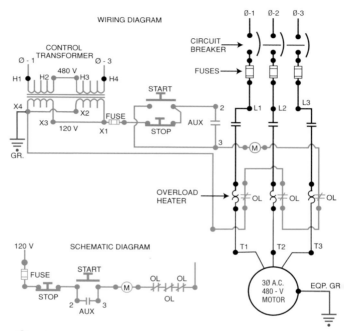

WIRING DIAGRAM

CONTROL TRANSFORMER

Ø-1   Ø-2   Ø-3

CIRCUIT BREAKER

FUSES

480 V
H1   H2   H3   H4

START

X4
X3   X2   FUSE
120 V   X1
GR.

STOP   AUX

2

L1   L2   L3

3

M

OVERLOAD HEATER

OL   OL   OL

120 V   SCHEMATIC DIAGRAM

T1   T2   T3

FUSE   START   OL   OL

STOP   M   OL

2   3
AUX

3Ø A.C.
480 - V
MOTOR

EQP. GR

(M) = MOTOR STARTER COIL

NOTE: CONTROLS AND MOTOR ARE OF DIFFERENT VOLTAGES.

- 46 -

TWO THREE WIRE STOP-START STATIONS

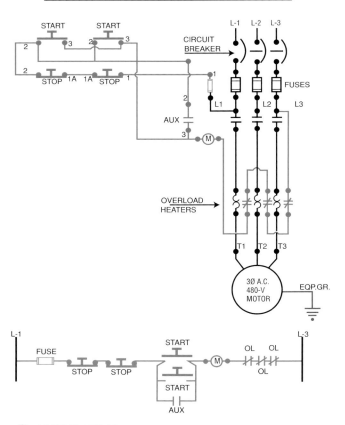

(M) = MOTOR STARTER COIL

Note: Controls and motor are of the same voltage.
       If Low Voltage controls are used, see UGLY'S page 46 for control
       transformer connections.

HAND OFF AUTOMATIC CONTROL

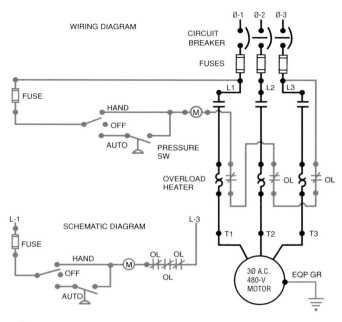

(M) = MOTOR STARTER COIL

Note: Controls and motor are of the same voltage.
         If Low Voltage controls are used, see UGLY'S page 46 for control
         transformer connections.

JOGGING WITH CONTROL RELAY

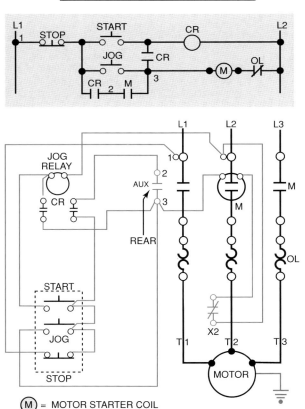

(M) = MOTOR STARTER COIL

Jogging circuits are used when machines must be operated momentarily for inching (as in set-up or maintenance). The jog circuit allows the starter to be energized only as long as the jog button is depressed.

VOLTAGE DROP CALCULATIONS
INDUCTANCE NEGLIGIBLE

Vd = Voltage Drop
I = Current in Conductor (Amperes)
L = One-way Length of Circuit (Ft.)
Cm = Cross Section Area of Conductor (Circular Mils) (page 71)
K = Resistance in ohms of one circular mil foot of conductor

K = 12.9 for Copper Conductors @75°C
K = 21.2 for Aluminum Conductors @75°C
NOTE: K value changes with temperature.
See NEC chapter 9, Table 8, Notes

SINGLE PHASE CIRCUITS:

$$Vd = \frac{2K \times L \times I}{Cm} \quad \text{or} \quad {}^*Cm = \frac{2K \times L \times I}{Vd}$$

THREE PHASE CIRCUITS:

$$Vd = \frac{1.73K \times L \times I}{Cm} \quad \text{or} \quad {}^*Cm = \frac{1.73K \times L \times I}{Vd}$$

* Note: Always check ampacity tables to insure conductors'
ampacity is equal to load <u>after voltage drop calculation</u>.

Refer to UGLY'S pages 71 - 78 for conductor size, type & ampacity.
See UGLY'S page 51 - 52 for examples.

VOLTAGE DROP EXAMPLES
DISTANCE (ONE-WAY) FOR 2% VOLTAGE DROP FOR <u>120 or 240 VOLTS</u> - SINGLE PHASE
(60°C insulation & terminals)

AMPS	VOLTS	12 AWG	10 AWG	8 AWG	6 AWG	4 AWG	3 AWG	2 AWG	1 AWG	1/0 AWG
20	120	30	48	77	122	194	245	309	389	491
	240	60	96	154	244	388	490	618	778	982
30	120		32	51	81	129	163	206	260	327
	240		64	102	162	258	326	412	520	654
40	120			38	61	97	122	154	195	246
	240			76	122	194	244	308	390	492
50	120				49	78	98	123	156	196
	240				98	156	196	246	312	392
60	120					65	82	103	130	164
60	240					130	164	206	260	328
70	240					111	140	176	222	281
80	240						122	154	195	246
90	240							137	173	218
100	240								156	196

(SEE FOOTNOTES PAGE 51 CONCERNING CIRCUIT LOAD LIMITATIONS)

VOLTAGE DROP EXAMPLES

Typical voltage drop values based on conductor size and one-way length* (60°C termination and insulation)

25 FEET								
		12 AWG	10 AWG	8 AWG	6 AWG	4 AWG	3 AWG	2 AWG	1 AWG
AMPERES	20	1.98	1.24	0.78	0.49	0.31	0.25	0.19	0.15
	30		1.86	1.17	0.74	0.46	0.37	0.29	0.23
	40			1.56	0.98	0.62	0.49	0.39	0.31
	50				1.23	0.77	0.61	0.49	0.39
	60					0.93	0.74	0.58	0.46

50 FEET								
		12 AWG	10 AWG	8 AWG	6 AWG	4 AWG	3 AWG	2 AWG	1 AWG
AMPERES	20	3.95	2.49	1.56	0.98	0.62	0.49	0.39	0.31
	30		3.73	2.34	1.47	0.93	0.74	0.58	0.46
	40			3.13	1.97	1.24	0.98	0.78	0.62
	50				2.46	1.55	1.23	0.97	0.77
	60					1.85	1.47	1.17	0.92

75 FEET								
		12 AWG	10 AWG	8 AWG	6 AWG	4 AWG	3 AWG	2 AWG	1 AWG
AMPERES	20	5.93	3.73	2.34	1.47	0.93	0.74	0.58	0.46
	30		5.59	3.52	2.21	1.39	1.10	0.87	0.69
	40			4.69	2.95	1.85	1.47	1.17	0.92
	50				3.69	2.32	1.84	1.46	1.16
	60					2.78	2.21	1.75	1.39

100 FEET								
		12 AWG	10 AWG	8 AWG	6 AWG	4 AWG	3 AWG	2 AWG	1 AWG
AMPERES	20	7.90	4.97	3.13	1.97	1.24	0.98	0.78	0.62
	30		7.46	4.69	2.95	1.85	1.47	1.17	0.92
	40			6.25	3.93	2.47	1.96	1.56	1.23
	50				4.92	3.09	2.45	1.94	1.54
	60					3.71	2.94	2.33	1.85

125 FEET								
		12 AWG	10 AWG	8 AWG	6 AWG	4 AWG	3 AWG	2 AWG	1 AWG
AMPERES	20	9.88	6.21	3.91	2.46	1.55	1.23	0.97	0.77
	30		9.32	5.86	3.69	2.32	1.84	1.46	1.16
	40			7.81	4.92	3.09	2.45	1.94	1.54
	50				6.15	3.86	3.06	2.43	1.93
	60					4.64	3.68	2.92	2.31

150 FEET								
		12 AWG	10 AWG	8 AWG	6 AWG	4 AWG	3 AWG	2 AWG	1 AWG
AMPERES	20	11.85	7.46	4.69	2.95	1.85	1.47	1.17	0.92
	30		11.18	7.03	4.42	2.78	2.21	1.75	1.39
	40			9.38	5.90	3.71	2.94	2.33	1.85
	50				7.37	4.64	3.68	2.92	2.31
	60					5.56	4.41	3.50	2.77

A two-wire 20-ampere circuit using 12 AWG with a one-way distance of 25 feet will drop 1.98 volts;
120 volts - 1.98 volts = 118.02 volts as the load voltage.
240 volts - 1.98 volts = 238.02 volts as the load voltage.

* Better economy and efficiency will result using the voltage drop method on page 50.
A continuous load cannot exceed 80% of the circuit rating.
A motor or heating load cannot exceed 80% of the circuit rating.
For motor overcurrent devices and conductor sizing, see page 41 - 42.

VOLTAGE DROP CALCULATIONS
EXAMPLES

SINGLE PHASE VOLTAGE DROP

What is the voltage drop of a 240 volt single phase circuit consisting of #8 THWN copper conductors feeding a 30 ampere load that is 150 feet in length?

Voltage Drop Formula - See UGLY'S page 50

$$Vd = \frac{2K \times L \times I}{Cm} = \frac{2 \times 12.9 \times 150 \times 30}{16,510} = \frac{116,100}{16,510} = 7 \text{ Volts}$$

Percentage voltage drop = 7 volts/240 volts = .029 = **2.9%**
Voltage at load = 240 volts - 7 volts = **233** volts

THREE PHASE VOLTAGE DROP

What is the voltage drop of a 480 volt three phase circuit consisting of 250 kcmil THWN copper conductors that supply a 250 ampere load that is 500 feet from the source?

Voltage Drop Formula - See UGLY'S page 50
250 kcmil = 250,000 circular mils

$$Vd = \frac{1.73K \times L \times I}{Cm} = \frac{1.73 \times 12.9 \times 500 \times 250}{250,000} = \frac{2,789,625}{250,000} = 11 \text{ Volts}$$

Percentage voltage drop = 11 volts/480 volts = .0229 = **2.29%**
Voltage at load = 480 volts - 11 volts = **469** volts

Note: Always check ampacity tables for conductors selected

Refer to UGLY'S pages 71 - 78 for conductor size, type & ampacity.

SHORT CIRCUIT CALCULATION

(Courtesy of Cooper Bussmann)

Basic Short-Circuit Calculation Procedure:

1. Determine transformer full-load amperes from either:
   a) Name plate
   b) Formula:

   3ø transf. $\quad I_{l.l.} = \dfrac{KVA \times 1000}{E_{L-L} \times 1.732}$

   1ø transf. $\quad I_{l.l.} = \dfrac{KVA \times 1000}{E_{L-L}}$

2. Find transformer multiplier.

   $$Multiplier = \frac{100}{*\%Z_{trans}}$$

3. Determine transformer let-thru short-circuit current.**

   $$I_{S.C.} = I_{l.l.} \times Multiplier$$

4. Calculate "f" factor.

   3Ø faults $\qquad f = \dfrac{1.732 \times L \times I_{3ø}}{C \times E_{L-L}}$

   1Ø line-to-line (L-L) faults $\quad f = \dfrac{2 \times L \times I_{L-L}}{C \times E_{L-L}}$
   on 1Ø Center Tapped
   Transformer

   1Ø line-to-neutral (L-N) $\quad f = \dfrac{2 \times L \times I_{L-N}{}^{***}}{C \times E_{L-N}}$
   faults on 1Ø Center Tapped
   Transformer

   L = length (feet) of conductor to the fault
   C = constant from Table C (page 55) for conductors & busway. For parallel runs, multiply C values by the number of conductors per phase.
   I = available short-circuit current in amperes at beginning of circuit.

5. Calculate "M" (multiplier) $\quad M = \dfrac{1}{1 + f}$

6. Calculate the available short-circuit symmetrical RMS current at the point of fault.

   $$I_{S.C.\ sym\ RMS} = I_{S.C.} \times M$$

(Continued - next page)

(Courtesy of Cooper Bussmann)

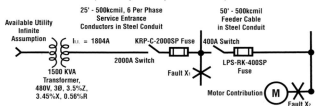

Example - Short-Circuit Calculation:
(FAULT #1)

1. $I_{l.l.} = \dfrac{\text{KVA} \times 1000}{E_{L-L} \times 1.732} = \dfrac{1500 \times 1000}{480 \times 1.732} = 1804 \text{ A}$

2. $\text{Multiplier} = \dfrac{100}{* \ \%Z_{trans}} = \dfrac{100}{3.5} = 28.57$

3. $I_{S.C.} = 1804 \times 28.57 = 51,540 \text{ A}$

4. $f = \dfrac{1.732 \times L \times I_{3\emptyset}}{C \times E_{L-L}} = \dfrac{1.73 \times 25 \times 51,540}{6 \times 22,185 \times 480} = 0.0349$

5. $M = \dfrac{1}{1 + f} = \dfrac{1}{1 + .0349} = .9663$

6. $I_{S.C. \text{ sym RMS}} = I_{S.C.} \times M = 51,540 \times .9663 = 49,803 \text{ A}$
   $I_{S.C. \text{ motor contrib}} = 4 \times 1,804 = 7,216 \text{ A}$
   $I_{total \ S.C. \text{ sym RMS}} = 49,803 + 7,216 = 57,019 \text{ A}$

(FAULT #2)

4. Use $I_{S.C. \text{ sym RMS}}$ @ Fault X_1 to calculate "f"

$f = \dfrac{1.73 \times 50 \times 49,803}{22,185 \times 480} = 0.4050$

5. $M = \dfrac{1}{1 + .4050} = .7117$

6. $I_{S.C. \text{ sym RMS}} = 49,803 \times .7117 = 35,445 \text{ A}$
   $I_{sym \text{ motor contrib}} = 4 \times 1,804 = 7,216 \text{ A}$
   $I_{total \ S.C. \text{ sym RMS}} = 35,445 + 7,216 = 42,661 \text{ A}$

 (Continued - next page)

TABLE "C"
"C" VALUES for CONDUCTORS (SHORT-CIRCUIT CALCULATION)
(Courtesy of Cooper Bussmann)

AWG or MCM	Copper Three Single Conductors Steel Conduit			Nonmagnetic Conduit			Copper Three Conductor Cable Steel Conduit			Nonmagnetic Conduit		
	600V	5KV	15KV	600V	5KV	15KV	600V	5KV	15KV	600V	5KV	15KV
12	617	617	617	617	617	617	617	617	617	617	617	617
10	981	981	981	981	981	981	981	981	981	981	981	981
8	1557	1551	1557	1558	1555	1558	1559	1557	1559	1559	1558	1559
6	2425	2406	2389	2430	2417	2406	2431	2424	2414	2433	2428	2420
4	3806	3750	3695	3825	3789	3752	3830	3811	3778	3837	3823	3798
3	4760	4760	4760	4802	4802	4802	4760	4790	4760	4802	4802	4802
2	5906	5736	5574	6044	5926	5809	5989	5929	5827	6087	6022	5957
1	7292	7029	6758	7493	7306	7108	7454	7364	7188	7579	7507	7364
1/0	8924	8543	7973	9317	9033	8590	9209	9086	8707	9472	9372	9052
2/0	10755	10061	9389	11423	10877	10318	11244	11045	10500	11703	11528	11052
3/0	12843	11804	11021	13923	13048	12360	13656	13333	12613	14410	14118	13461
4/0	15082	13605	12542	16673	15351	14347	16391	15890	14813	17482	17019	16012
250	16483	14924	13643	18593	17120	15865	18310	17850	16465	19779	19352	18001
300	18176	16292	14768	20867	18975	17408	20617	20051	18318	22524	21938	20163
350	19703	17385	15678	22736	20526	18672	22646	21914	19821	24904	24126	21982
400	20565	18235	16365	24296	21786	19731	24253	23371	21042	26915	26044	23517
500	22185	19172	17492	26706	23277	21329	26980	25449	23125	30028	28712	25916
600	22965	20567	17962	28033	25203	22097	28752	27954	24896	32236	31258	27766
750	24136	21386	18888	28303	25430	22690	31050	30024	26932	32404	31338	28303
1000	25278	22539	19923	31490	28083	24887	33864	32688	29320	37197	35748	31959

SHORT-CIRCUIT CALCULATION *(continued)*
(Courtesy of Cooper Bussmann)

NOTES:

* Transformer impedance (Z) helps to determine what the short circuit current will be at the transformer secondary. Transformer impedance is determined as follows: The transformer secondary is short circuited. Voltage is applied to the primary which causes full load current to flow in the secondary. This applied voltage divided by the rated primary voltage is the impedance of the transformer.

Example:

For a 480 volt rated primary, if 9.6 volts causes secondary full load current to flow through the shorted secondary, the transformer impedance is $9.6 \div 480 = .02 = 2\%Z$. In addition, U.L. listed transformers 25KVA and larger have a ± 10% impedance tolerance. Short circuit amperes can be affected by this tolerance.

** Motor Short-circuit contribution, if significant, may be added to the transformer secondary short-circuit current value as determined in Step 3. Proceed with this adjusted figure through Steps 4,5 and 6. A practical estimate of motor short-circuit contribution is to multiply the total motor current in amperes by 4.

*** The L-N fault current is higher than the L-L fault current at the secondary terminals of a single-phase center-tapped transformer. The short-circuit current available (I) for this case in Step 4 should be adjusted at the transformer terminals as follows: At L-N center tapped transformer terminals,

I_{L-N} = 1.5 x I_{L-L} **at Transformer Terminals.**

COMPONENT PROTECTION
HOW TO USE CURRENT-LIMITATION CHARTS
(Courtesy of Cooper Bussmann)

Example: 800A circuit and an 800A Low-Peak current-limiting time-delay fuse

How to Use the Let-Through Charts:
Using the example above, one can determine the pertinent let-through data for the KRP-C-800SP amp Low-Peak fuse. The Let-Through Chart pertaining to the 800A Low-Peak fuse is illustrated.

A. Determine the PEAK let-through CURRENT.
1. Enter the chart on the Prospective Short-Circuit Current scale at 86,000 amps and proceed vertically until the 800A fuse curve is intersected.
2. Follow horizontally until the Instantaneous Peak Let-Through Current scale is intersected.
3. Read the PEAK let-through CURRENT as 49,000A. (If a fuse had not been used, the peak current would have been 198,000A.)

B. Determine the APPARENT PROSPECTIVE RMS SYMMETRICAL let-through CURRENT.
1. Enter the chart on the Prospective Short-Circuit current scale at 86,000A and proceed vertically until the 800A fuse curve is intersected.
2. Follow horizontally until line A-B is intersected.
3. Proceed vertically down to the Prospective Short-Circuit Current.
4. Read the APPARENT PROSPECTIVE RMS SYMMETRICAL let-through CURRENT as 21,000A. (The RMS SYMMETRICAL let-through CURRENT would be 86,000A if there were no fuse in the circuit.)

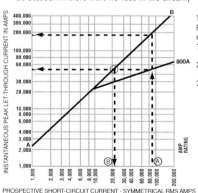

The data that can be obtained from the Fuse Let-Through Charts and their physical effects are:
1) Peak let-through current: mechanical forces
2) Apparent prospective RMS symmetrical let-through current: heating effect
3) Clearing time: less than 1/2 cycle when fuse is in its current-limiting range (beyond where fuse curve intersects A-B line)

Ⓐ I_{RMS} Available = **86,000 Amps**
Ⓑ I_{RMS} Let-Through = **21,000 Amps**
Ⓒ I_p Available = **198,000 Amps**
Ⓓ I_p Let-Through = **49,000 Amps**

PROSPECTIVE SHORT-CIRCUIT CURRENT - SYMMETRICAL RMS AMPS

Reprinted with permission, copyright 2006, Cooper Bussmann; www.cooperbussmann.com;

SINGLE-PHASE TRANSFORMER CONNECTIONS

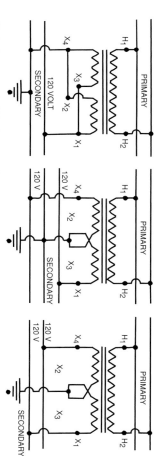

Single-phase to supply 120 volt lighting load. Often used for single lighting customer.

Single-phase to supply 120/240 - 3 wire lighting and power load. Used in urban distribution circuits.

Single-phase for power. Used for small industrial applications.

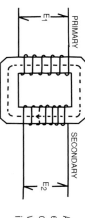

SINGLE Ø TRANSFORMER CIRCUIT

A transformer is a stationary induction device for transferring electrical energy from one circuit to another without change of frequency. A transformer consists of two coils or windings wound upon a magnetic core of soft iron laminations, and insulated from one another.

- 58 -

BUCK AND BOOST TRANSFORMER CONNECTIONS

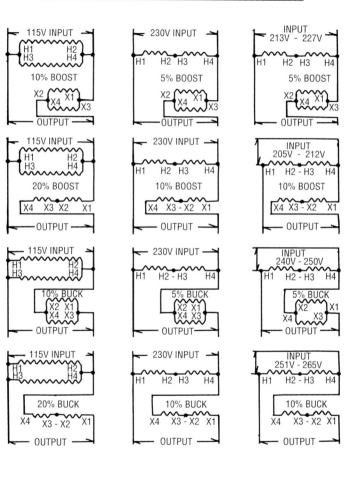

- 59 -

FULL LOAD CURRENTS

THREE-PHASE TRANSFORMERS VOLTAGE (LINE TO LINE)

$$I = \frac{KVA \times 1000}{E \times 1.73} \quad \text{or} \quad KVA = \frac{E \times I \times 1.73}{1000}$$

KVA RATING	208	240	480	2400	4160
3	8.3	7.2	3.6	.72	.416
6	16.7	14.4	7.2	1.44	.83
9	25.0	21.7	10.8	2.17	1.25
15	41.6	36.1	18.0	3.6	2.08
30	83.3	72.2	36.1	7.2	4.16
45	124.9	108.3	54.1	10.8	6.25
75	208.2	180.4	90.2	18.0	10.4
100	277.6	240.6	120.3	24.1	13.9
150	416.4	360.9	180.4	36.1	20.8
225	624.6	541.3	270.6	54.1	31.2
300	832.7	721.7	360.9	72.2	41.6
500	1387.9	1202.8	601.4	120.3	69.4
750	2081.9	1804.3	902.1	180.4	104.1
1000	2775.8	2405.7	1202.8	240.6	138.8
1500	4163.7	3608.5	1804.3	360.9	208.2
2000	5551.6	4811.4	2405.7	481.1	277.6
2500	6939.5	6014.2	3007.1	601.4	347.0
5000	13879.0	12028.5	6014.2	1202.8	694.0
7500	20818.5	18042.7	9021.4	1804.3	1040.9
10000	27758.0	24057.0	12028.5	2405.7	1387.9

SINGLE-PHASE TRANSFORMERS VOLTAGE

$$I = \frac{KVA \times 1000}{E} \quad \text{or} \quad KVA = \frac{E \times I}{1000}$$

KVA RATING	120	208	240	480	2400
1	8.33	4.81	4.17	2.08	.42
3	25.0	14.4	12.5	6.25	1.25
5	41.7	24.0	20.8	10.4	2.08
7.5	62.5	36.1	31.3	15.6	3.13
10	83.3	48.1	41.7	20.8	4.17
15	125.0	72.1	62.5	31.3	6.25
25	208.3	120.2	104.2	52.1	10.4
37.5	312.5	180.3	156.3	78.1	15.6
50	416.7	240.4	208.3	104.2	20.8
75	625.0	360.6	312.5	156.3	31.3
100	833.3	480.8	416.7	208.3	41.7
125	1041.7	601.0	520.8	260.4	52.1
167.5	1395.8	805.3	697.9	349.0	69.8
200	1666.7	961.5	833.3	416.7	83.3
250	2083.3	1201.9	1041.7	520.8	104.2
333	2775.0	1601.0	1387.5	693.8	138.8
500	4166.7	2403.8	2083.3	1041.7	208.3

TRANSFORMER CALCULATIONS

To better understand the following formulas, review the rule of transposition in equations.

A multiplier may be removed from one side of an equation by making it a divisor on the other side; or a divisor may be removed from one side of an equation by making it a multiplier on the other side.

1. VOLTAGE AND CURRENT: PRIMARY (p) AND SECONDARY (s)

POWER (p) = POWER (s) or $E_p \times I_p = E_s \times I_s$

A. $E_p = \dfrac{E_s \times I_s}{I_p}$

B. $I_p = \dfrac{E_s \times I_s}{E_p}$

C. $\dfrac{E_p \times I_p}{E_s} = I_s$

D. $\dfrac{E_p \times I_p}{I_s} = E_s$

2. VOLTAGE AND TURNS IN COIL:

VOLTAGE (p) × TURNS (s) = VOLTAGE (s) × TURNS (p)

or

$E_p \times T_s = E_s \times T_p$

A. $E_p = \dfrac{E_s \times T_p}{T_s}$

B. $T_s = \dfrac{E_s \times T_p}{E_p}$

C. $\dfrac{E_p \times T_s}{E_s} = T_p$

D. $\dfrac{E_p \times T_s}{T_p} = E_s$

3. AMPERES AND TURNS IN COIL:

AMPERES (p) × TURNS (p) = AMPERES (s) × TURNS (s)

or

$I_p \times T_p = I_s \times T_s$

A. $I_p = \dfrac{I_s \times T_s}{T_p}$

B. $T_p = \dfrac{I_s \times T_s}{I_p}$

C. $\dfrac{I_p \times T_p}{I_s} = T_s$

D. $\dfrac{I_p \times T_p}{T_s} = I_s$

SIZING TRANSFORMERS

SINGLE PHASE TRANSFORMERS:

Size a 480-volt-primary/240/120-volt secondary single-phase transformer for the following single-phase incandescent lighting load consisting of 48 recessed fixtures each rated 2 amperes, 120-volt. Each fixture has a 150-watt lamp.
* (These fixtures can be evenly balanced on the transformer)

Find total volt-amperes using fixture ratings -
do not use lamp watt rating.

> 2 amperes x 120-volts = 240-volt-amperes
> 240-va x 48 = 11,520va
> 11,520va/1000 = 11.52 KVA

The single-phase transformer that meets or exceeds this value is **15 KVA**.

* 24 lighting fixtures would be connected line one to the common neutral and 24 lighting fixtures would be connected line two to the common neutral.

THREE-PHASE TRANSFORMERS:

Size a 480-volt primary/240-volt secondary three-phase transformer (Poly-phase unit) to supply one three-phase 25 KVA process heater and one single-phase 5 KW unit heater.

The 5KW unit heater can not be balanced across all three phases. The 5 KW will be on one phase only. Adding the loads directly will undersize the transformer. Common practice is to put an imaginary load equal to the single-phase load on the other two phases.
5 KW x 3 = 15 KW*
The 25 KVA is three-phase; use 25 KVA.
25 KVA + 15 KVA* = 40 KVA.
The nearest three-phase transformer that meets or exceeds this value is a **45 KVA**.
* (KVA = KW at unity power factor) (Transformers are rated in KVA)

SINGLE PHASE TRANSFORMER
PRIMARY & SECONDARY AMPERES

A 480/240-volt single phase 50 KVA transformer (Z=2%) is to be installed. Calculate primary and secondary amperes, and short circuit amperes.

PRIMARY AMPERES:

$$Ip = \frac{KVA \times 1000}{Ep} = \frac{50 \times 1000}{480} = \frac{50,000}{480} = \textbf{104 AMPERES}$$

SECONDARY AMPERES:

$$Is = \frac{KVA \times 1000}{Es} = \frac{50 \times 1000}{240} = \frac{50,000}{240} = \textbf{208 AMPERES}$$

SHORT CIRCUIT AMPERES:*

$$Isc = \frac{Is}{\%Z} = \frac{208}{.02} = \textbf{10,400 AMPERES}$$

THREE PHASE TRANSFORMER
PRIMARY & SECONDARY AMPERES

A 480/208-volt three phase 100 KVA transformer (Z=1%) is to be installed. Calculate primary and secondary amperes, and short circuit amperes.

PRIMARY AMPERES:

$$Ip = \frac{KVA \times 1000}{Ep \times 1.73} = \frac{100 \times 1000}{480 \times 1.73} = \frac{100,000}{831} = \textbf{120 AMPERES}$$

SECONDARY AMPERES:

$$Is = \frac{KVA \times 1000}{Es \times 1.73} = \frac{100 \times 1000}{208 \times 1.73} = \frac{100,000}{360} = \textbf{278 AMPERES}$$

SHORT CIRCUIT AMPERES:*

$$Isc = \frac{Is}{\%Z} = \frac{208}{.01} = \textbf{27,800 AMPERES}$$

* Short circuit amperes is the current that would flow if the transformers' secondary terminals were shorted phase to phase. See UGLY'S page 53 for calculating short circuit amperes point to point using the Cooper Bussmann method.

THREE PHASE CONNECTIONS

WYE (STAR)

Voltage from "A", "B", or "C" to Neutral = E_{PHASE} (E_P)

Voltage between A-B, B-C, or C-A = E_{LINE} (E_L)

I_L = I_P, if balanced.

If unbalanced,

$$I_N = \sqrt{I_A^2 + I_B^2 + I_C^2 - (I_A \times I_B) - (I_B \times I_C) - (I_C \times I_A)}$$

E_L = E_P x 1.73

E_P = E_L ÷ 1.73

(True Power)
Power =

    I_L x E_L x 1.73 x Power Factor
                (cosine)

(Apparent Power)
Voltamperes = I_L x E_L x 1.73

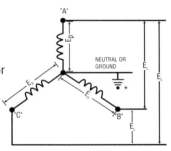

DELTA

E_{LINE} (E_L) = E_{PHASE} (E_P)

I_{LINE} = I_P x 1.73

I_{PHASE} = I_L ÷ 1.73

(True Power)
Power =

    I_L x E_L x 1.73 x Power Factor
                (cosine)

(Apparent Power)
Voltamperes = I_L x E_L x 1.73

* Neutral could be ungrounded
Also see NEC A250 System
Grounding Requirements

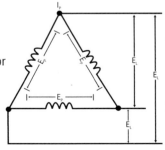

THREE-PHASE STANDARD PHASE ROTATION

TRANSFORMERS

STAR-DELTA

STAR-STAR

DELTA-DELTA

ADDITIVE POLARITY
30° ANGULAR-DISPLACEMENT

SUBTRACTIVE POLARITY
0° PHASE-DISPLACEMENT

SUBTRACTIVE POLARITY
0° PHASE-DISPLACEMENT

TRANSFORMER CONNECTIONS

SERIES CONNECTIONS OF LOW VOLTAGE WINDINGS

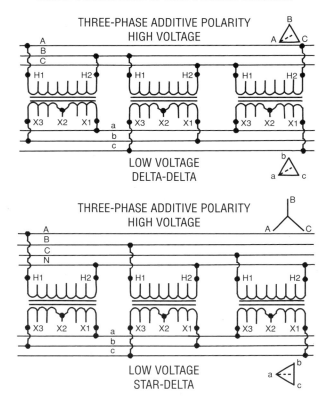

THREE-PHASE ADDITIVE POLARITY
HIGH VOLTAGE

LOW VOLTAGE
DELTA-DELTA

THREE-PHASE ADDITIVE POLARITY
HIGH VOLTAGE

LOW VOLTAGE
STAR-DELTA

NOTE: Single-phase transformers should be thoroughly checked
for impedance, polarity, and voltage ratio before installation.

TRANSFORMER CONNECTIONS

SERIES CONNECTIONS OF LOW VOLTAGE WINDINGS

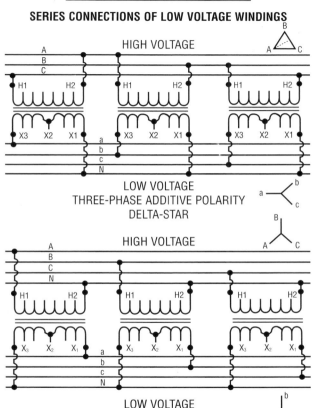

HIGH VOLTAGE

LOW VOLTAGE
THREE-PHASE ADDITIVE POLARITY
DELTA-STAR

HIGH VOLTAGE

LOW VOLTAGE
THREE-PHASE ADDITIVE POLARITY
STAR-STAR

NOTE: For additive polarity the H-1 and the X-1 bushings are diagonally opposite each other.

TRANSFORMER CONNECTIONS

SERIES CONNECTIONS OF LOW VOLTAGE WINDINGS

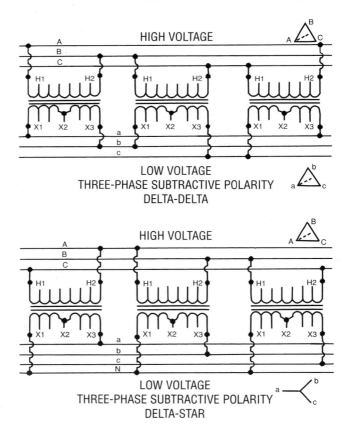

HIGH VOLTAGE

LOW VOLTAGE
THREE-PHASE SUBTRACTIVE POLARITY
DELTA-DELTA

HIGH VOLTAGE

LOW VOLTAGE
THREE-PHASE SUBTRACTIVE POLARITY
DELTA-STAR

NOTE: For subtractive polarity the H-1 and the X-1 bushings are
directly opposite each other.

MISCELLANEOUS WIRING DIAGRAMS

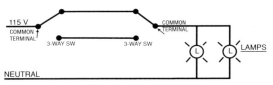

TWO 3-WAY SWITCHES

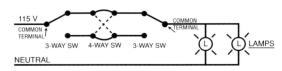

**TWO 3-WAY SWITCHES
ONE 4-WAY SWITCH**

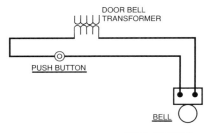

BELL CIRCUIT

MISCELLANEOUS WIRING DIAGRAMS

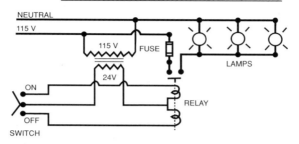

REMOTE CONTROL CIRCUIT - ONE RELAY AND ONE SWITCH

SUPPORTS FOR RIGID METAL CONDUIT

CONDUIT SIZE	DISTANCE BETWEEN SUPPORTS
1/2" - 3/4"	10 FEET
1"	12 FEET
1-1/4" - 1-1/2"	14 FEET
2" - 2-1/2"	16 FEET
3" AND LARGER	20 FEET

SUPPORT OF RIGID NONMETALLIC CONDUIT

CONDUIT SIZE	DISTANCE BETWEEN SUPPORTS
1/2" - 1"	3 FEET
1-1/4" - 2"	5 FEET
2-1/2" - 3"	6 FEET
3-1/2" - 5"	7 FEET
6"	8 FEET

For SI units: (Supports) one foot = 0.3048 meter

CONDUCTOR PROPERTIES

| Size | Area | Conductors | | | | DC Resistance at 75°C (167°F) | | |
| | | Stranding | | Overall | | Copper | | Aluminum |
AWG/ kcmil	Cir. Mils	Quan- tity	Diam. In.	Diam. In.	Area In²	Uncoated ohm/kFT	Coated ohm/kFT	ohm/ kFT
18	1620	1	----	0.040	0.001	7.77	8.08	12.8
18	1620	7	0.015	0.046	0.002	7.95	8.45	13.1
16	2580	1	----	0.051	0.002	4.89	5.08	8.05
16	2580	7	0.019	0.058	0.003	4.99	5.29	8.21
14	4110	1	----	0.064	0.003	3.07	3.19	5.06
14	4110	7	0.024	0.073	0.004	3.14	3.26	5.17
12	6530	1	----	0.081	0.005	1.93	2.01	3.18
12	6530	7	0.030	0.092	0.006	1.98	2.05	3.25
10	10380	1	----	0.102	0.008	1.21	1.26	2.00
10	10380	7	0.038	0.116	0.011	1.24	1.29	2.04
8	16510	1	----	0.128	0.013	0.764	0.786	1.26
8	16510	7	0.049	0.146	0.017	0.778	0.809	1.28
6	26240	7	0.061	0.184	0.027	0.491	0.510	0.808
4	41740	7	0.077	0.232	0.042	0.308	0.321	0.508
3	52620	7	0.087	0.260	0.053	0.245	0.254	0.403
2	66360	7	0.097	0.292	0.067	0.194	0.201	0.319
1	83690	19	0.066	0.332	0.087	0.154	0.160	0.253
1/0	105600	19	0.074	0.372	0.109	0.122	0.127	0.201
2/0	133100	19	0.084	0.418	0.137	0.0967	0.101	0.159
3/0	167800	19	0.094	0.470	0.173	0.0766	0.0797	0.126
4/0	211600	19	0.106	0.528	0.219	0.0608	0.0626	0.100
250	----	37	0.082	0.575	0.260	0.0515	0.0535	0.0847
300	----	37	0.090	0.630	0.312	0.0429	0.0446	0.0707
350	----	37	0.097	0.681	0.364	0.0367	0.0382	0.0605
400	----	37	0.104	0.728	0.416	0.0321	0.0331	0.0529
500	----	37	0.116	0.813	0.519	0.0258	0.0265	0.0424
600	----	61	0.099	0.893	0.626	0.0214	0.0223	0.0353
700	----	61	0.107	0.964	0.730	0.0184	0.0189	0.0303
750	----	61	0.111	0.998	0.782	0.0171	0.0176	0.0282
800	----	61	0.114	1.030	0.834	0.0161	0.0166	0.0265
900	----	61	0.122	1.094	0.940	0.0143	0.0147	0.0235
1000	----	61	0.128	1.152	1.042	0.0129	0.0132	0.0212
1250	----	91	0.117	1.289	1.305	0.0103	0.0106	0.0169
1500	----	91	0.128	1.412	1.566	0.00858	0.00883	0.0141
1750	----	127	0.117	1.526	1.829	0.00735	0.00756	0.0121
2000	----	127	0.126	1.632	2.092	0.00643	0.00662	0.0106

These resistance values are valid ONLY for the parameters as given. Using conductors having coated strands, different stranding type, and, especially, other temperatures changes the resistance.

Formula for temperature change: $R_2 = R_1 [1 + \alpha(T_2 - 75)]$ where $\alpha_{cu} = 0.00323$, $\alpha_{AL} = 0.00330$ at 75°C.

See NEC Chapter 9, Table 8.   See Ugly's page 130 - 138 for metric conversions.

AC Resistance and Reactance for 600 Volt Cables, 3-Phase, 60 Hz, 75°C (167°F) – Three Single Conductors in Conduit

Ohms to Neutral per 1000 Feet

Size AWG/ kcmil	X_L (Reactance) for All Wires		AC Resistance for Uncoated Copper Wires			AC Resistance for Aluminum Wires			Effective Z at 0.85 PF for Uncoated Copper Wires			Effective Z at 0.85 PF for Aluminum Wires			Size AWG/ kcmil
	PVC, Al. Conduit	Steel Conduit	PVC Conduit	Al. Conduit	Steel Conduit	PVC Conduit	Al. Conduit	Steel Conduit	PVC Conduit	Al. Conduit	Steel Conduit	PVC Conduit	Al. Conduit	Steel Conduit	
14	0.058	0.073	3.1	3.1	3.1	–	–	–	2.7	2.7	2.7	–	–	–	14
12	0.054	0.068	2.0	2.0	2.0	3.2	3.2	3.2	1.7	1.7	1.7	2.8	2.8	2.8	12
10	0.050	0.063	1.2	1.2	1.2	2.0	2.0	2.0	1.1	1.1	1.1	1.8	1.8	1.8	10
8	0.052	0.065	0.78	0.78	0.78	1.3	1.3	1.3	0.69	0.69	0.70	1.1	1.1	1.1	8
6	0.051	0.064	0.49	0.49	0.49	0.81	0.81	0.81	0.44	0.45	0.45	0.71	0.72	0.72	6
4	0.048	0.060	0.31	0.31	0.31	0.51	0.51	0.51	0.29	0.30	0.30	0.46	0.46	0.46	4
3	0.047	0.059	0.25	0.25	0.25	0.40	0.41	0.40	0.23	0.24	0.24	0.37	0.37	0.37	3
2	0.045	0.057	0.19	0.20	0.20	0.32	0.32	0.32	0.19	0.19	0.20	0.30	0.30	0.30	2
1	0.046	0.057	0.15	0.16	0.16	0.25	0.26	0.25	0.16	0.16	0.16	0.24	0.24	0.25	1
1/0	0.044	0.055	0.12	0.13	0.12	0.20	0.21	0.20	0.13	0.13	0.13	0.19	0.20	0.20	1/0
2/0	0.043	0.054	0.10	0.10	0.10	0.16	0.16	0.16	0.11	0.11	0.11	0.16	0.16	0.16	2/0
3/0	0.042	0.052	0.077	0.082	0.079	0.13	0.13	0.13	0.088	0.092	0.094	0.13	0.14	0.14	3/0
4/0	0.041	0.051	0.062	0.067	0.063	0.10	0.11	0.10	0.074	0.078	0.080	0.11	0.11	0.11	4/0
250	0.041	0.052	0.052	0.057	0.054	0.085	0.090	0.086	0.066	0.070	0.073	0.094	0.098	0.10	250
300	0.041	0.051	0.044	0.049	0.045	0.071	0.076	0.072	0.059	0.063	0.065	0.082	0.086	0.088	300
350	0.040	0.050	0.038	0.043	0.039	0.061	0.066	0.063	0.053	0.058	0.060	0.073	0.077	0.080	350
400	0.040	0.049	0.033	0.038	0.035	0.054	0.059	0.055	0.049	0.053	0.056	0.066	0.071	0.073	400
500	0.039	0.048	0.027	0.032	0.029	0.043	0.048	0.045	0.043	0.048	0.050	0.057	0.061	0.064	500
600	0.039	0.048	0.023	0.028	0.025	0.036	0.041	0.038	0.040	0.044	0.047	0.051	0.055	0.058	600
750	0.038	0.048	0.019	0.024	0.021	0.029	0.034	0.031	0.036	0.040	0.043	0.045	0.049	0.052	750
1000	0.037	0.046	0.015	0.019	0.018	0.023	0.027	0.025	0.032	0.036	0.040	0.039	0.042	0.046	1000

Notes: See NEC Table 9, page 70-568 for assumptions and explanations.
See Ugly's page 130 - 138 for metric conversion.

ALLOWABLE AMPACITIES OF CONDUCTORS

Allowable Ampacities of Insulated Conductors Rated 0 - 2000 Volts, 60°C Through 90°C (140°F Through 194°F), **Not More Than Three Current-Carrying Conductors** in **Raceway, Cable, or Earth** (Directly Buried), Based on Ambient Air Temperature of 30°C (86°F)

SIZE	60°C (140°F)	75°C (167°F)	90°C (194°F)	60°C (140°F)	75°C (167°F)	90°C (194°F)	SIZE
AWG or kcmil	TYPES TW, UF	TYPES RHW, THHW, THW, THWN, XHHW, USE, ZW	TYPES TBS, SA, SIS, FEP, FEPB, MI, RHH, RHW-2, THHN, THHW, THW-2,THWN-2, USE-2,XHH, XHHW, XHHW-2, ZW-2	TYPES TW, UF	TYPES RHW, THHW, THW, THWN, XHHW, USE	TYPES TBS, SA, SIS, THHN, THHW, THW-2, THWN-2, RHH, RHW-2, USE-2, XHH, XHHW, XHHW-2, ZW-2	AWG or kcmil
	COPPER			ALUMINUM OR COPPER-CLAD ALUMINUM			
14*	20	20	25	----	----	----	14
12*	25	25	30	20	20	25	12*
10*	30	35	40	25	30	35	10*
8	40	50	55	30	40	45	8
6	55	65	75	40	50	60	6
4	70	85	95	55	65	75	4
3	85	100	110	65	75	85	3
2	95	115	130	75	90	100	2
1	110	130	150	85	100	115	1
1/0	125	150	170	100	120	135	1/0
2/0	145	175	195	115	135	150	2/0
3/0	165	200	225	130	155	175	3/0
4/0	195	230	260	150	180	205	4/0
250	215	255	290	170	205	230	250
300	240	285	320	190	230	255	300
350	260	310	350	210	250	280	350
400	280	335	380	225	270	305	400
500	320	380	430	260	310	350	500
600	355	420	475	285	340	385	600
700	385	460	520	310	375	420	700
750	400	475	535	320	385	435	750
800	410	490	555	330	395	450	800
900	435	520	585	355	425	480	900
1000	455	545	615	375	445	500	1000
1250	495	590	665	405	485	545	1250
1500	520	625	705	435	520	585	1500
1750	545	650	735	455	545	615	1750
2000	560	665	750	470	560	630	2000

Ambient Temp C°	TEMPERATURE CORRECTION FACTORS For ambient temperatures other than 30°C, multiply the allowable ampacities shown above by the appropriate factor shown below.						Ambient Temp F°
21 - 25	1.08	1.05	1.04	1.08	1.05	1.04	70 - 77
26 - 30	1.00	1.00	1.00	1.00	1.00	1.00	78 - 86
31 - 35	0.91	0.94	0.96	0.91	0.94	0.96	87 - 95
36 - 40	0.82	0.88	0.91	0.82	0.88	0.91	96 - 104
41 - 45	0.71	0.82	0.87	0.71	0.82	0.87	105 - 113
46 - 50	0.58	0.75	0.82	0.58	0.75	0.82	114 - 122
51 - 55	0.41	0.67	0.76	0.41	0.67	0.76	123 - 131
56 - 60	——	0.58	0.71	——	0.58	0.71	132 - 140
61 - 70	——	0.33	0.58	——	0.33	0.58	141 - 158
71 - 80	——	——	0.41	——	——	0.41	159 - 176

See UGLY'S page 77 for Footnotes to this page, Overcurrent Protection (Fuses and Circuit Breakers), Adjustment Factors based on Number of Conductors, Adjustment Examples and copyright notice. See NEC 240.4(D).

ALLOWABLE AMPACITIES OF CONDUCTORS

Allowable Ampacities of **Single Insulated Conductors** Rated 0 - 2000 Volts in **Free Air**, Based on Ambient Air Temperature of **30°C** (86°F)

SIZE	60°C (140°F)	75°C (167°F)	90°C (194°F)	60°C (140°F)	75°C (167°F)	90°C (194°F)	SIZE
AWG or kcmil	TYPES TW, UF	TYPES RHW, THHW, THW, THWN, XHHW, ZW	TYPES TBS, SA, SIS, FEP, FEPB, MI, RHH, RHW-2, THHN, THHW, THW-2,THWN-2, USE-2, XHH, XHHW, XHHW-2, ZW-2	TYPES TW, UF	TYPES RHW, THHW, THW, THWN, XHHW,	TYPES TBS, SA, SIS, THHN, THHW, THW-2, THWN-2, RHH, RHW-2, USE-2, XHH, XHHW, XHHW-2, ZW-2	AWG or kcmil
			COPPER		ALUMINUM OR COPPER-CLAD ALUMINUM		
14*	25	30	35	----	----	----	14
12*	30	35	40	25	30	35	12*
10*	40	50	55	35	40	40	10*
8	60	70	80	45	55	60	8
6	80	95	105	60	75	80	6
4	105	125	140	80	100	110	4
3	120	145	165	95	115	130	3
2	140	170	190	110	135	150	2
1	165	195	220	130	155	175	1
1/0	195	230	260	150	180	205	1/0
2/0	225	265	300	175	210	235	2/0
3/0	260	310	350	200	240	275	3/0
4/0	300	360	405	235	280	315	4/0
250	340	405	455	265	315	355	250
300	375	445	505	290	350	395	300
350	420	505	570	330	395	445	350
400	455	545	615	355	425	480	400
500	515	620	700	405	485	545	500
600	575	690	780	455	540	615	600
700	630	755	855	500	595	675	700
750	655	785	885	515	620	700	750
800	680	815	920	535	645	725	800
900	730	870	985	580	700	785	900
1000	780	935	1055	625	750	845	1000
1250	890	1065	1200	710	855	960	1250
1500	980	1175	1325	795	950	1075	1500
1750	1070	1280	1445	875	1050	1185	1750
2000	1155	1385	1560	960	1150	1335	2000

Ambient Temp C°	TEMPERATURE CORRECTION FACTORS For ambient temperatures other than 30°C, multiply the allowable ampacities shown above by the appropriate factor shown below.						Ambient Temp F°
21 - 25	1.08	1.05	1.04	1.08	1.05	1.04	70 - 77
26 - 30	1.00	1.00	1.00	1.00	1.00	1.00	78 - 86
31 - 35	0.91	0.94	0.96	0.91	0.94	0.96	87 - 95
36 - 40	0.82	0.88	0.91	0.82	0.88	0.91	96 - 104
41 - 45	0.71	0.82	0.87	0.71	0.82	0.87	105 - 113
46 - 50	0.58	0.75	0.82	0.58	0.75	0.82	114 - 122
51 - 55	0.41	0.67	0.76	0.41	0.67	0.76	123 - 131
56 - 60	——	0.58	0.71	——	0.58	0.71	132 - 140
61 - 70	——	0.33	0.58	——	0.33	0.58	141 - 158
71 - 80	——	——	0.41	——	——	0.41	159 - 176

See UGLY'S page 77 for Footnotes to this page, Overcurrent Protection (Fuses and Circuit Breakers), Adjustment Factors based on Number of Conductors, Adjustment Examples and copyright statement. See NEC 240.4(D).

ALLOWABLE AMPACITIES OF CONDUCTORS

Allowable Ampacities of Insulated Conductors Rated 0 - 2000 Volts, 150°C Through 250°C (302°F Through 482°F), **Not More Than Three Current-Carrying Conductors** in **Raceway or Cable**, Based on Ambient Air Temperature of **40°C (104°F)**

SIZE	150°C (302°F)	200°C (392°F)	250°C (482°F)	150°C (302°F)	SIZE
	TYPE Z	TYPES FEP, FEPB, PFA, SA	TYPES PFAH, TFE	TYPE Z	
AWG or kcmil					AWG or kcmil
	COPPER		NICKEL or NICKEL-COATED COPPER	ALUMINUM or COPPER-CLAD ALUMINUM	
14	34	36	39	---	14
12	43	45	54	30	12
10	55	60	73	44	10
8	76	83	93	57	8
6	96	110	117	75	6
4	120	125	148	94	4
3	143	152	166	109	3
2	160	171	191	124	2
1	186	197	215	145	1
1/0	215	229	244	169	1/0
2/0	251	260	273	198	2/0
3/0	288	297	308	227	3/0
4/0	332	346	361	260	4/0
Ambient Temp C°	TEMPERATURE CORRECTION FACTORS For ambient temperatures other than **40°C**, multiply the allowable ampacities shown above by the appropriate factor shown below.				Ambient Temp F°
41 - 50	0.95	0.97	0.98	0.95	105 - 122
51 - 60	0.90	0.94	0.95	0.90	123 - 140
61 - 70	0.85	0.90	0.93	0.85	141 - 158
71 - 80	0.80	0.87	0.90	0.80	159 - 176
81 - 90	0.74	0.83	0.87	0.74	177 - 194
91 - 100	0.67	0.79	0.85	0.67	195 - 212
101 - 120	0.52	0.71	0.79	0.52	213 - 248
121 - 140	0.30	0.61	0.72	0.30	249 - 284
141 - 160	----	0.50	0.65	----	285 - 320
161 - 180	---	0.35	0.58	---	321 - 356
181 - 200	---	---	0.49	---	357 - 392
201 - 225	---	---	0.35	---	393 - 437

ALLOWABLE AMPACITIES OF CONDUCTORS

Allowable Ampacities of **Single Insulated Conductors**, Rated 0 - 2000 Volts, 150°C Through 250°C (302°F Through 482°F), **in Free Air**, Based on Ambient Air Temperature of **40°C (104°F)**					
SIZE	150°C (302°F)	200°C (392°F)	250°C (482°F)	150°C (302°F)	SIZE
	TYPE Z	TYPES FEP, FEPB, PFA, SA	TYPES PFAH, TFE	TYPE Z	
AWG or kcmil					AWG or kcmil
	COPPER		NICKEL or NICKEL-COATED COPPER	ALUMINUM or COPPER-CLAD ALUMINUM	
14	46	54	59	---	14
12	60	68	78	47	12
10	80	90	107	63	10
8	106	124	142	83	8
6	155	165	205	112	6
4	190	220	278	148	4
3	214	252	327	170	3
2	255	293	381	198	2
1	293	344	440	228	1
1/0	339	399	532	263	1/0
2/0	390	467	591	305	2/0
3/0	451	546	708	351	3/0
4/0	529	629	830	411	4/0
Ambient Temp C°	**TEMPERATURE CORRECTION FACTORS** For ambient temperatures other than **40°C**, multiply the allowable ampacities shown above by the appropriate factor shown below.				Ambient Temp F°
41 - 50	0.95	0.97	0.98	0.95	105 - 122
51 - 60	0.90	0.94	0.95	0.90	123 - 140
61 - 70	0.85	0.90	0.93	0.85	141 - 158
71 - 80	0.80	0.87	0.90	0.80	159 - 176
81 - 90	0.74	0.83	0.87	0.74	177 - 194
91 - 100	0.67	0.79	0.85	0.67	195 - 212
101 - 120	0.52	0.71	0.79	0.52	213 - 248
121 - 140	0.30	0.61	0.72	0.30	249 - 284
141 - 160	----	0.50	0.65	----	285 - 320
161 - 180	---	0.35	0.58	---	321 - 356
181 - 200	---	---	0.49	---	357 - 392
201 - 225	---	---	0.35	---	393 - 437

Unless specifically permitted in 240.4(E) or 240.4(G), the overcurrent protection shall not exceed 15 amperes for 14 AWG, 20 amperes for 12 AWG, and 30 amperes for 10 AWG copper; or 15 amperes for 12 AWG and 25 amperes for 10 AWG aluminum and copper-clad aluminum after any correction factors for ambient temperature and number of conductors have been applied. (See NEC 240.4(D) for 18 and 16 AWG Copper.)

AMPACITY CORRECTION AND ADJUSTMENT FACTORS
EXAMPLES

UGLY'S page 73 shows ampacity values for not more than three current-carrying conductors in a raceway or cable and an ambient (surrounding) temperature of 30˚C (86˚F).

(Example 1) A raceway contains three #3 THWN conductors for a three phase circuit at an ambient temperature of 30˚C.
UGLY'S page 73, 75˚ column indicates **100 amperes**.

(Example 2) A raceway contains three #3 THWN conductors for a three phase circuit at an ambient temperature of 40˚C. UGLY'S page 73, 75˚ column indicates **100 amperes**. This value must be corrected for ambient temperature (see Temperature Correction Factors at bottom of UGLY'S page 73). 40˚C factor is **.88**
100 amperes x .88 = **88 amperes** = corrected ampacity

(Example 3) A raceway contains six #3 THWN conductors for two three phase circuits at an ambient temperature of 30˚C.
UGLY'S page 73, 75˚ column indicates **100 amperes**. This value must be adjusted for more than three current-carrying conductors. The Table on UGLY'S page 78 requires an adjustment of **80%** for four through six current-carrying conductors. 100 amperes x 80% = **80** amperes
The adjusted ampacity is **80 amperes**

(Example 4) A raceway contains six #3 THWN conductors for two three phase circuits in an ambient temperature of 40˚C. These conductors must be derated for both temperature and number of conductors.
UGLY'S page 73, 75˚ column indicates **100** amperes
UGLY'S page 73, 40˚C temperature factor is **.88**
UGLY'S page 78, 4 - 6 conductor factor is **.80**
100 amperes x .88 x .80 = **70.4** amperes
The new derated ampacity is **70.4 amperes**.

ADJUSTMENT FACTORS
for More than Three Current-Carrying Conductors in a Raceway or Cable

Number of Current-Carrying Conductors	Percent of Values in Tables 310-16 through 310-19 as Adjusted for Ambient Temperature if Necessary
4 - 6	80
7 - 9	70
10 - 20	50
21 - 30	45
31 - 40	40
41 and above	35

CONDUCTOR AND EQUIPMENT TERMINATION RATINGS*
EXAMPLES

A 150-ampere circuit breaker is labeled for 75°C terminations and is selected to be used for a 150-ampere non-continuous load. It would be permissible to use a 1/0 THWN conductor that has a 75°C insulation rating and has an ampacity of 150 amperes. (Ugly's page 73).

When a THHN (90°C) conductor is connected to a 75°C termination, it is limited to the 75°C ampacity. Therefore, if a 1 THHN conductor with a rating of 150 amperes were connected to a 75°C terminal, its ampacity would be limited to 130-amperes instead of 150-amperes, which is too small for the load. (Ugly's page 73).

If the 150-ampere non-continuous load listed above uses 1/0 THWN conductors rated 150 amperes and the conductors are in an ambient temperature of 40°C, the conductors would have to be corrected for the ambient temperature.

From Ugly's page 74, 40°C temperature correction factor = **.88**
1/0 THWN = 150 amperes
150 amperes x .88 = **132 amperes** (which is too small for the load, so a larger size conductor is required).

Apply temperature correction factors to the next size THWN conductor.
2/0 THWN = 175 amperes (from the 75°C column - Ugly's page 74)
175 amperes x .88 = **154 amperes**. This size is suitable for the 150-ampere load.

The advantage of using 90°C conductors is that you can apply ampacity derating factors to the higher 90°C ampacity rating, and it may save you from going to a larger conductor. *(continued next page)*

CONDUCTOR AND EQUIPMENT TERMINATION RATINGS*

(continued from page 78)

1/0 THHN = 170 amperes (from the 90°C column - Ugly's page 73).
40°C temperature correction factor = .91 (90°C column - Ugly's page 73).
170 amperes x .91 = **154.7 amperes**.
This size is suitable for the 150-ampere load.
This 90°C conductor can be used but can never have a final derated ampacity over the rating of 1/0 THWN 75°C rating of 150 amperes.

You are allowed to use higher temperature insulated conductors such as THHN (90°C) conductors on 60°C or 75°C terminals of circuit breakers and equipment, and you are allowed to derate from the higher value for temperature and number of conductors, but the final derated ampacity is limited to the 60°C or 75°C terminal insulation labels.

* See NEC 2008 Article 110.14(C1)(C2)

CONDUCTOR APPLICATIONS AND INSULATIONS

TRADE NAME	LETTER	MAX. TEMP.	APPLICATION PROVISIONS
FLOURINATED ETHYLENE PROPYLENE	FEP OR FEPB	90°C 194°F 200°C 392°F	DRY AND DAMP LOCATIONS DRY LOCATIONS - SPECIAL APPLICATIONS[2]
MINERAL INSULATION (METAL SHEATHED)	MI	90°C 194°F 250°C 482°F	DRY AND WET LOCATIONS SPECIAL APPLICATIONS[2]
MOISTURE, HEAT-, AND OIL-RESISTANT THERMOPLASTIC	MTW	60°C 140°F 90°C 194°F	MACHINE TOOL WIRING IN WET LOCATIONS MACHINE TOOL WIRING IN DRY LOCATIONS, FPN: See NFPA 79
PAPER		85°C 185°F	FOR UNDERGROUND SERVICE CONDUCTORS, OR BY SPECIAL PERMISSION
PERFLUORO-ALKOXY	PFA	90°C 194°F 200°C 392°F	DRY AND DAMP LOCATIONS DRY LOCATIONS - SPECIAL APPLICATIONS[2]

SEE *UGLY'S* PAGE 82 FOR SPECIAL PROVISIONS AND/OR APPLICATIONS.

CONDUCTOR APPLICATIONS AND INSULATIONS

TRADE NAME	LETTER	MAX. TEMP.	APPLICATION PROVISIONS
PERFLUORO-ALKOXY	PFAH	250°C 482°F	DRY LOCATIONS ONLY. ONLY FOR LEADS WITHIN APPARATUS OR WITHIN RACEWAYS CONNECTED TO APPARATUS, (NICKEL OR NICKEL-COATED COPPER ONLY).
THERMOSET	RHH	90°C 194°F	DRY AND DAMP LOCATIONS
MOISTURE-RESISTANT THERMOSET	RHW[4]	75°C 167°F	DRY & WET LOCATIONS
MOISTURE-RESISTANT THERMOSET	RHW-2	90°C 194°F	DRY AND WET LOCATIONS
SILICONE	SA	90°C 194°F 200°C 392°F	DRY AND DAMP LOCATIONS FOR SPECIAL APPLICATIONS[2]
THERMOSET	SIS	90°C 194°F	SWITCHBOARD WIRING ONLY
THERMOPLASTIC AND FIBROUS OUTER BRAID	TBS	90°C 194°F	SWITCHBOARD WIRING ONLY
EXTENDED POLYTETRAFLUORO-ETHYLENE	TFE	250°C 482°F	DRY LOCATIONS ONLY. ONLY FOR LEADS WITHIN APPARATUS OR WITH-IN RACEWAYS CONNECTED TO APPA-RATUS, OR AS OPEN WIRING (NIC-KEL OR NICKEL-COATED COPPER ONLY).
HEAT-RESISTANT THERMOPLASTIC	THHN	90°C 194°F	DRY AND DAMP LOCATIONS
MOISTURE-AND HEAT-RESISTANT THERMOPLASTIC	THHW	75°C 167°F 90°C 194°F	WET LOCATION DRY LOCATION

SEE *UGLY'S* PAGE 82 FOR SPECIAL PROVISIONS AND/OR APPLICATIONS.

CONDUCTOR APPLICATIONS AND INSULATIONS

TRADE NAME	LETTER	MAX. TEMP.	APPLICATION PROVISIONS
MOISTURE - AND HEAT-RESISTANT THERMOPLASTIC	THW	75°C 167°F	DRY & WET LOCATIONS
		90°C 194°F	SPECIAL APPL. WITHIN ELECTRIC DISCHARGE LIGHTING EQUIPMENT. LIMITED TO 1000 OPEN-CIRCUIT VOLTS OR LESS, (SIZE 14-8 ONLY AS PERMITTED IN SECTION 410-33)
	THW-2	90°C 194°F	DRY AND WET LOCATIONS
MOISTURE - AND HEAT-RESISTANT THERMOPLASTIC	THWN	75°C 167°F	DRY AND WET LOCATIONS
	THWN-2	90°C 194°F	
MOISTURE-RESISTANT THERMOPLASTIC	TW	60°C 140°F	DRY AND WET LOCATIONS
UNDERGROUND FEEDER AND BRANCH-CIRCUIT CABLE-SINGLE CONDUCTOR, (FOR TYPE "UF" CABLE EMPLOYING MORE THAN 1 CONDUCTOR. (SEE NEC ART. 340)	UF	60°C 140°F 75°C 167°F[7]	SEE ARTICLE 340 N.E.C.
UNDERGROUND SERVICE-ENTRANCE CABLE-SINGLE CONDUCTOR, (FOR TYPE "USE" CABLE EMPLOYING MORE THAN 1 CONDUCTOR. SEE N.E.C. ART. 338)	USE	75°C 167°F	SEE ARTICLE 338 N.E.C.
	USE-2	90°C 194°F	DRY AND WET LOCATIONS

SEE *UGLY'S* PAGE 82 FOR SPECIAL PROVISIONS AND/OR APPLICATIONS.

CONDUCTOR APPLICATIONS AND INSULATIONS

TRADE NAME	LETTER	MAX. TEMP.	APPLICATION PROVISIONS
THERMOSET	XHH	90°C 194°F	DRY AND DAMP LOCATIONS
MOISTURE-RESISTANT THERMOSET	XHHW[4]	90°C 194°F	DRY AND DAMP LOCATIONS
		75°C 167°F	WET LOCATIONS
MOISTURE-RESISTANT THERMOSET	XHHW-2	90°C 194°F	DRY AND WET LOCATIONS
MODIFIED ETHYLENE TETRAFLUORO-ETHYLENE	Z	90°C 194°F	DRY AND DAMP LOCATIONS
		150°C 302°F	DRY LOCATIONS - SPECIAL APPLICATIONS[2]
MODIFIED ETHYLENE TETRAFLUORO-ETHYLENE	ZW	75°C 167°F	WET LOCATIONS
		90°C 194°F	DRY AND DAMP LOCATIONS
		150°C 302°F	DRY LOCATIONS - SPECIAL APPLICATIONS[2]
	ZW-2	90°C 194°F	DRY AND WET LOCATIONS

FOOTNOTES:

1 Some insulations do not require an outer covering.

2 Where design conditions require maximum conductor operating temperatures above 90°C (194°F).

3 For signaling circuits permitting 300-volt insulation.

4 Some rubber insulations do not require an outer covering.

5 Includes integral jacket.

6 For ampacity limitation, see Section 340.80 NEC.

7 Insulation thickness shall be permitted to be 2.03 mm (80 mils) for listed Type USE conductors that have been subjected to special investigations. The non-metallic covering over individual rubber-covered conductors of aluminum-sheathed cable and of lead-sheathed or multiconductor cable shall not be required to be flame retardant. For Type MC cable, see 330.104. For nonmetallic-sheathed cable, see Article 334, Part III. For Type UF cable, see Article 340, Part III.

MAXIMUM NUMBER OF CONDUCTORS IN TRADE SIZES OF CONDUIT OR TUBING

The 2008 National Electrical Code© shows 85 tables for conduit fill. There is a separate table for each type of conduit. In order to keep Ugly's Electrical References© in a compact and easy to use format, the following tables are included:

Electrical Metallic Tubing (EMT), Electrical Nonmetallic Tubing (ENT),

PVC 40, PVC 80, Rigid Metal Conduit, Flexible Metal Conduit and Liquidtight Flexible Metal Conduit.

When other types of conduit are used, refer to Appendix C2002 *NEC* or use method shown below to figure conduit size.

Example #1 - All same wire size and type insulation.
10 – #12 RHH in Intermediate Metal Conduit.
Go to the RHH Conductor Square Inch Area Table. (Ugly's page 98)
#12 RHH = .0353 sq. in.   10 x .0353 sq. in. = .353 sq. in.
Go to Intermediate Metal Conduit Square Inch Area Table. (Ugly's page 101)
Use "Over 2 Wires 40%" column.
³/₄ inch conduit = .235 sq. in. (less than .353, so it's too small).
1 inch conduit = .384 sq. in. (greater than .353, so it's correct size).

Example #2 - Different wire sizes or types insulation.
10 – #12 RHH and 10 – #10 THHN in Liquidtight Nonmetallic Conduit (LFNC-B).
Go to the RHH Conductor Square Inch Area Table. (Ugly's page 98)
#12 RHH = .0353 sq. in.   10 x .0353 sq. in. = .353 sq. in.
Go to the THHN Conductor Square Inch Area Table. (Ugly's page 98)
#10 THHN = .0211 sq. in.   10 x .0211 sq. in. = .211 sq. in.
.353 sq. in. + .211 sq. in. = .564 sq. in.
Go to Liquidtight Nonmetallic Conduit (LFNC-B) Square Inch Table. (Ugly's page 102)
Use "Over 2 Wires 40%" column.
1 inch conduit = .349 sq. in. (less than .564, so it's too small).
1¹/₄ inch conduit = .611 sq. in. (greater than .564, so it's correct size).

NOTE 1*: All conductors must be counted including grounding conductors for fill percentage.
NOTE 2: When all conductors are same type and size, decimals .8 and larger must be rounded up.
NOTE 3**: These are minimum size calculations, under certain conditions jamming can occur and the next size conduit must be used.
NOTE 4***: CAUTION - When over three current carrying conductors are used in same circuit, conductor ampacity must be lower (derated).

*   See Appendix C and Chapter Nine 2002 NEC for complete tables and examples.
**   See Chapter nine Table one and Notes 1 - 10, 2002 NEC.
*** See notes to Ampacity Tables, Note 8, 2002 NEC.

MAXIMUM NUMBER OF CONDUCTORS IN *ELECTRICAL METALLIC TUBING*

Type Letters	Cond. Size AWG/kcmil	Trade Sizes In Inches									
		½	¾	1	1¼	1½	2	2½	3	3½	4
RHH, RHW, RHW-2	14	4	7	11	20	27	46	80	120	157	201
	12	3	6	9	17	23	38	66	100	131	167
	10	2	5	8	13	18	30	53	81	105	135
	8	1	2	4	7	9	16	28	42	55	70
	6	1	1	3	5	8	13	22	34	44	56
	4	1	1	2	4	6	10	17	26	34	44
	3	1	1	1	4	5	9	15	23	30	38
	2	1	1	1	3	4	7	13	20	26	33
	1	0	1	1	1	3	5	9	13	17	22
	1/0	0	1	1	1	2	4	7	11	15	19
	2/0	0	1	1	1	2	4	6	10	13	17
	3/0	0	0	1	1	1	3	5	8	11	14
	4/0	0	0	1	1	1	3	5	7	9	12
	250	0	0	0	1	1	1	3	5	7	9
	300	0	0	0	1	1	1	3	5	6	8
	350	0	0	0	1	1	1	3	4	6	7
	400	0	0	0	1	1	1	2	4	5	7
	500	0	0	0	0	1	1	2	3	4	6
	600	0	0	0	0	1	1	1	3	4	5
	700	0	0	0	0	0	1	1	3	3	4
	750	0	0	0	0	0	1	1	2	3	4
TW,	14	8	15	25	43	58	96	168	254	332	424
	12	6	11	19	33	45	74	129	195	255	326
	10	5	8	14	24	33	55	96	145	190	243
	8	2	5	8	13	18	30	53	81	105	135
RHH*, RHW*, RHW-2*, THHW, THW, THW-2	14	6	10	16	28	39	64	112	169	221	282
RHH*, RHW*, RHW-2*, THHW, THW	12	4	8	13	23	31	51	90	136	177	227
	10	3	6	10	18	24	40	70	106	138	177
RHH*, RHW*, RHW-2*, THHW, THW, THW-2	8	1	4	6	10	14	24	42	63	83	106
RHH*, RHW*, RHW-2*, TW, THW, THHW. THW-2	6	1	3	4	8	11	18	32	48	63	81
	4	1	1	3	6	8	13	24	36	47	60
	3	1	1	3	5	7	12	20	31	40	52
	2	1	1	2	4	6	10	17	26	34	44
	1	1	1	1	3	4	7	12	18	24	31
	1/0	0	1	1	2	3	6	10	16	20	26
	2/0	0	1	1	1	3	5	9	13	17	22
	3/0	0	1	1	1	2	4	7	11	15	19
	4/0	0	0	1	1	1	3	6	9	12	16
	250	0	0	1	1	1	3	5	7	10	13
	300	0	0	1	1	1	2	4	6	8	11
	350	0	0	0	1	1	1	4	6	7	10
	400	0	0	0	1	1	1	3	5	7	9
	500	0	0	0	0	1	1	3	4	6	7
	600	0	0	0	0	1	1	2	3	4	6
	700	0	0	0	0	1	1	1	3	4	5
	750	0	0	0	0	1	1	1	3	4	5
THHN, THWN, THWN-2	14	12	22	35	61	84	138	241	364	476	608
	12	9	16	26	45	61	101	176	266	347	443
	10	5	10	16	28	38	63	111	167	219	279
	8	3	6	9	16	22	36	64	96	126	161
	6	2	4	7	12	16	26	46	69	91	116
	4	1	2	4	7	10	16	28	43	56	71
	3	1	1	3	6	8	13	24	36	47	60
	2	1	1	3	5	7	11	20	30	40	51
	1	1	1	1	4	5	8	15	22	29	37

Reprinted with permission from NFPA 70-2008, the *National Electrical Code*®, Copyright 2007, National Fire Protection Association, Quincy, MA 02269. This reprinted material is not the referenced subject which is represented only by the Standard in its entirety.

MAXIMUM NUMBER OF CONDUCTORS IN *ELECTRICAL METALLIC TUBING*

Type Letters	Cond. Size AWG/kcmil	Trade Sizes In Inches									
		1/2	3/4	1	1 1/4	1 1/2	2	2 1/2	3	3 1/2	4
THHN, THWN, THWN-2	1/0	1	1	1	3	4	7	12	19	25	32
	2/0	0	1	1	2	3	6	10	16	20	26
	3/0	0	1	1	1	3	5	8	13	17	22
	4/0	0	1	1	1	2	4	7	11	14	18
	250	0	0	1	1	1	3	6	9	11	15
	300	0	0	1	1	1	3	5	7	10	13
	350	0	0	1	1	1	2	5	6	9	11
	400	0	0	0	1	1	1	4	6	8	10
	500	0	0	0	1	1	1	3	5	6	8
	600	0	0	0	0	1	1	1	4	5	7
	700	0	0	0	0	1	1	1	2	4	6
	750	0	0	0	0	0	1	1	3	4	5
FEP, FEPB, PFA, PFAH, TFE	14	12	21	34	60	81	134	234	354	462	590
	12	9	15	25	43	59	98	171	258	337	430
	10	6	11	18	31	42	70	122	185	241	309
	8	3	6	10	18	24	40	70	106	138	177
	6	2	4	7	12	17	28	50	75	98	126
	4	1	3	5	9	12	20	35	53	69	88
	3	1	2	4	7	10	16	29	44	57	73
	2	1	1	3	6	8	13	24	36	47	60
PFA, PFAH, TFE	1	1	1	2	4	6	9	16	25	33	42
PFAH, TFE PFA, TFE, Z	1/0	1	1	1	3	5	8	14	21	27	35
	2/0	0	1	1	3	4	6	11	17	22	29
	3/0	0	1	1	2	3	5	9	14	18	24
	4/0	0	1	1	1	2	4	8	11	15	19
Z	14	14	25	41	72	98	161	282	426	556	711
	12	10	18	29	51	69	114	200	302	394	504
	10	6	11	18	31	42	70	122	185	241	309
	8	4	7	11	20	27	44	77	117	153	195
	6	3	5	8	14	19	31	54	82	107	137
	4	1	3	5	9	13	21	37	56	74	94
	3	1	2	4	7	9	15	27	41	54	69
	2	1	1	3	6	8	13	22	34	45	57
	1	1	1	2	4	6	10	18	28	36	46
XHH, XHHW, XHHW-2, ZW	14	8	15	25	43	58	96	168	254	332	424
	12	6	11	19	33	45	74	129	195	255	326
	10	5	8	14	24	33	55	96	145	190	243
	8	2	5	8	13	18	30	53	81	105	135
	6	1	3	6	10	14	22	39	60	78	100
	4	1	2	4	7	10	16	28	43	56	72
	3	1	1	3	6	8	14	24	36	48	61
	2	1	1	3	5	7	11	20	31	40	51
XHH, XHHW, XHHW-2	1	1	1	1	4	5	8	15	23	30	38
	1/0	1	1	1	3	4	7	13	19	25	32
	2/0	0	1	1	2	3	6	10	16	21	27
	3/0	0	1	1	1	3	5	9	13	17	22
	4/0	0	1	1	1	2	4	7	11	14	18
	250	0	0	1	1	1	3	6	9	12	15
	300	0	0	1	1	1	3	5	8	10	13
	350	0	0	1	1	1	2	4	7	9	11
	400	0	0	0	1	1	1	4	6	8	10
	500	0	0	0	1	1	1	3	5	6	8
	600	0	0	0	1	1	1	2	4	5	6
	700	0	0	0	0	1	1	2	3	4	6
	750	0	0	0	0	1	1	1	3	4	5

* Types RHH, RHW, AND RHW-2 without outer covering.

See Ugly's page 134 for Trade Size / Metric Designator conversion.

MAXIMUM NUMBER OF CONDUCTORS IN *NONMETALLIC TUBING*

Type Letters	Cond. Size AWG/kcmil	Trade Sizes In Inches					
		1/2	3/4	1	1 1/4	1 1/2	2
RHH, RHW, RHW-2	14	3	6	10	19	26	43
	12	2	5	9	16	22	36
	10	1	4	7	13	17	29
	8	1	1	3	6	9	15
	6	1	1	3	5	7	12
	4	1	1	2	4	6	9
	3	1	1	1	3	5	8
	2	0	1	1	3	4	7
	1	0	1	1	1	3	5
	1/0	0	0	1	1	2	4
	2/0	0	0	1	1	1	3
	3/0	0	0	1	1	1	3
	4/0	0	0	1	1	1	2
	250	0	0	0	1	1	1
	300	0	0	0	1	1	1
	350	0	0	0	1	1	1
	400	0	0	0	1	1	1
	500	0	0	0	0	1	1
	600	0	0	0	0	1	1
	700	0	0	0	0	0	1
	750	0	0	0	0	0	1
TW	14	7	13	22	40	55	92
	12	5	10	17	31	42	71
	10	4	7	13	23	32	52
	8	1	4	7	13	17	29
RHH*, RHW*, RHW-2*, THHW, THW, THW-2	14	4	8	15	27	37	61
RHH*, RHW*, RHW-2*, THHW, THW	12	3	7	12	21	29	49
	10	3	5	9	17	23	38
RHH*, RHW*, RHW-2*, THHW, THW, THW-2	8	1	3	5	10	14	23
RHH*, RHW*, RHW-2*, TW, THW, THHW, THW-2	6	1	2	4	7	10	17
	4	1	1	3	5	8	13
	3	1	1	2	5	7	11
	2	1	1	2	4	6	9
	1	0	1	1	3	4	6
	1/0	0	1	1	2	3	5
	2/0	0	1	1	1	3	5
	3/0	0	0	1	1	2	4
	4/0	0	0	1	1	1	3
	250	0	0	1	1	1	2
	300	0	0	0	1	1	2
	350	0	0	0	1	1	1
	400	0	0	0	1	1	1
	500	0	0	0	1	1	1
	600	0	0	0	0	1	1
	700	0	0	0	0	1	1
	750	0	0	0	0	1	1
THHN, THWN, THWN-2	14	10	18	32	58	80	132
	12	7	13	23	42	58	96
	10	4	8	15	26	36	60
	8	2	5	8	15	21	35
	6	1	3	6	11	15	25
	4	1	1	4	7	9	15
	3	1	1	3	5	8	13
	2	1	1	2	5	6	11
	1	1	1	1	3	5	8

MAXIMUM NUMBER OF CONDUCTORS IN *NONMETALLIC TUBING*

Type Letters	Cond. Size AWG/kcmil	Trade Sizes In Inches					
		1/2	3/4	1	1 1/4	1 1/2	2
THHN, THWN, THWN-2	1/0	0	1	1	3	4	7
	2/0	0	1	1	2	3	5
	3/0	0	1	1	1	3	4
	4/0	0	0	1	1	2	4
	250	0	0	1	1	1	3
	300	0	0	1	1	1	2
	350	0	0	0	1	1	2
	400	0	0	0	1	1	1
	500	0	0	0	1	1	1
	600	0	0	0	1	1	1
	700	0	0	0	1	1	1
	750	0	0	0	0	1	1
FEP, FEPB, PFA, PFAH, TFE	14	10	18	31	56	77	128
	12	7	13	23	41	56	93
	10	5	9	16	29	40	67
	8	3	5	9	17	23	38
	6	1	4	6	12	16	27
	4	1	2	4	8	11	19
	3	1	1	4	7	9	16
	2	1	1	3	5	8	13
PFA, PFAH, TFE	1	1	1	1	4	5	9
PFAH, TFE PFA, TFE, Z	1/0	0	1	1	3	4	7
	2/0	0	1	1	2	4	6
	3/0	0	1	1	1	3	5
	4/0	0	1	1	1	2	4
Z	14	12	22	38	68	93	154
	12	8	15	27	48	66	109
	10	5	9	16	29	40	67
	8	3	6	10	18	25	42
	6	1	4	7	13	18	30
	4	1	3	5	9	12	20
	3	1	1	3	6	9	15
	2	1	1	3	5	7	12
	1	1	1	2	4	6	10
XHH, XHHW, XHHW-2, ZW	14	7	13	22	40	55	92
	12	5	10	17	31	42	71
	10	4	7	13	23	32	52
	8	1	4	7	13	17	29
	6	1	3	5	9	13	21
	4	1	1	4	7	9	15
	3	1	1	3	6	8	13
	2	1	1	2	5	6	11
XHH, XHHW, XHHW-2	1	1	1	1	3	5	8
	1/0	0	1	1	3	4	7
	2/0	0	1	1	2	3	6
	3/0	0	1	1	1	3	5
	4/0	0	0	1	1	2	4
	250	0	0	0	1	1	3
	300	0	0	1	1	1	3
	350	0	0	0	1	1	2
	400	0	0	0	1	1	1
	500	0	0	0	1	1	1
	600	0	0	0	1	1	1
	700	0	0	0	0	1	1
	750	0	0	0	0	1	1

* Types RHH, RHW, AND RHW-2 without outer covering.

See Ugly's page 134 for Trade Size / Metric Designator conversion.

Reprinted with permission from NFPA 70-2008, the *National Electrical Code*®, Copyight 2007, National Fire Protection Association, Quincy, MA 02269. This reprinted material is not the referenced subject which is represented only by the Standard in its entirety.

MAXIMUM NUMBER OF CONDUCTORS IN *RIGID PVC CONDUIT, SCHEDULE 40*

Type Letters	Cond. Size AWG/kcmil	Trade Sizes In Inches											
		½	¾	1	1¼	1½	2	2½	3	3½	4	5	6
RHH, RHW, RHW-2	14	4	7	11	20	27	45	64	99	133	171	269	390
	12	3	5	9	16	22	37	53	82	110	142	224	323
	10	2	4	7	13	18	30	43	66	89	115	181	261
	8	1	2	4	7	9	15	22	35	46	60	94	137
	6	1	1	3	5	7	12	18	28	37	48	76	109
	4	1	1	2	4	6	10	14	22	29	37	59	85
	3	1	1	1	4	5	8	12	19	25	33	52	75
	2	1	1	1	3	4	7	10	16	22	28	45	65
	1	0	1	1	1	3	5	7	11	14	19	29	43
	1/0	0	1	1	1	2	4	6	9	13	16	26	37
	2/0	0	0	1	1	1	3	5	8	11	14	22	32
	3/0	0	0	1	1	1	3	4	7	9	12	19	28
	4/0	0	0	1	1	1	2	4	6	8	10	16	24
	250	0	0	0	1	1	1	3	4	6	8	12	18
	300	0	0	0	1	1	1	2	4	5	7	11	16
	350	0	0	0	1	1	1	2	3	5	6	10	14
	400	0	0	0	1	1	1	1	3	4	6	9	13
	500	0	0	0	0	1	1	1	3	4	5	8	11
	600	0	0	0	0	1	1	1	2	3	4	6	9
	700	0	0	0	0	0	1	1	1	3	3	6	8
	750	0	0	0	0	0	1	1	1	2	3	5	8
TW	14	8	14	24	42	57	94	135	209	280	361	568	822
	12	6	11	18	32	44	72	103	160	215	277	436	631
	10	4	8	13	24	32	54	77	119	160	206	325	470
	8	2	4	7	13	18	30	43	66	89	115	181	261
RHH*, RHW*, RHW-2*, THHW, THW, THW-2	14	5	9	16	28	38	63	90	139	186	240	378	546
RHH*, RHW*, RHW-2*, THHW, THW	12	4	8	12	22	30	50	72	112	150	193	304	439
	10	3	6	10	17	24	39	56	87	117	150	237	343
RHH*, RHW*, RHW-2*, THHW, THW, THW-2	8	1	3	6	10	14	23	33	52	70	90	142	205
RHH*, RHW*, RHW-2*, TW, THW, THHW, THW-2	6	1	2	4	8	11	18	26	40	53	69	109	157
	4	1	1	3	6	8	13	19	30	40	51	81	117
	3	1	1	3	5	7	11	16	25	34	44	69	100
	2	1	1	2	4	6	10	14	22	29	37	59	85
	1	0	1	1	3	4	7	10	15	20	26	41	60
	1/0	0	1	1	2	3	6	8	13	17	22	35	51
	2/0	0	1	1	1	3	5	7	11	15	19	30	43
	3/0	0	1	1	1	2	4	6	9	12	16	25	36
	4/0	0	0	1	1	1	3	5	8	10	13	21	30
	250	0	0	1	1	1	3	4	6	8	11	17	25
	300	0	0	1	1	1	2	3	5	7	9	15	21
	350	0	0	0	1	1	1	3	5	6	8	13	19
	400	0	0	0	1	1	1	3	4	6	7	12	17
	500	0	0	0	1	1	1	2	3	5	6	10	14
	600	0	0	0	0	1	1	1	3	4	5	8	11
	700	0	0	0	0	1	1	1	2	3	4	7	10
	750	0	0	0	0	1	1	1	2	3	4	6	10
THHN, THWN, THWN-2	14	11	21	34	60	82	135	193	299	401	517	815	1178
	12	8	15	25	43	59	99	141	218	293	377	594	859
	10	5	9	15	27	37	62	89	137	184	238	374	541
	8	3	5	9	16	21	36	51	79	106	137	216	312
	6	1	4	6	11	15	26	37	57	77	99	156	225
	4	1	2	4	7	9	16	22	35	47	61	96	138
	3	1	1	3	6	8	13	19	30	40	51	81	117
	2	1	1	3	5	7	11	16	25	33	43	68	98
	1	1	1	1	3	5	8	12	18	25	32	50	73

MAXIMUM NUMBER OF CONDUCTORS IN *RIGID PVC CONDUIT, SCHEDULE 40*

Type Letters	Cond. Size AWG/kcmil	Trade Sizes In Inches											
		1/2	3/4	1	1 1/4	1 1/2	2	2 1/2	3	3 1/2	4	5	6
THHN, THWN, THWN-2	1/0	1	1	1	3	4	7	10	15	21	27	42	61
	2/0	0	1	1	2	3	6	8	13	17	22	35	51
	3/0	0	1	1	1	3	5	7	11	14	18	29	42
	4/0	0	1	1	1	2	4	6	9	12	15	24	35
	250	0	0	1	1	1	3	4	7	10	12	20	28
	300	0	0	1	1	1	3	4	6	8	11	17	24
	350	0	0	1	1	1	2	3	5	7	9	15	21
	400	0	0	0	1	1	1	3	5	6	8	13	19
	500	0	0	0	1	1	1	2	4	5	7	11	16
	600	0	0	0	1	1	1	1	3	4	5	9	13
	700	0	0	0	0	1	1	1	3	4	5	8	11
	750	0	0	0	0	1	1	1	3	3	4	7	11
FEP, FEPB, PFA, PFAH, TFE	14	11	20	33	58	79	131	188	290	389	502	790	1142
	12	8	15	24	42	58	96	137	212	284	366	577	834
	10	6	10	17	30	41	69	98	152	204	263	414	598
	8	3	6	10	17	24	39	56	87	117	150	237	343
	6	2	4	7	12	17	28	40	62	83	107	169	244
	4	1	3	5	8	12	19	28	43	58	75	118	170
	3	1	2	4	7	10	16	23	36	48	62	98	142
	2	1	1	3	6	8	13	19	30	40	51	81	117
PFA, PFAH, TFE	1	1	1	2	4	5	9	13	20	28	36	56	81
PFA, PFAH, TFE, Z	1/0	1	1	1	3	4	7	8	11	17	23	30	47	68
	2/0	0	1	1	3	4	6	9	14	19	24	39	56
	3/0	0	1	1	2	3	5	7	12	16	20	32	46
	4/0	0	1	1	1	2	4	6	9	13	16	26	38
Z	14	13	24	40	70	95	158	226	350	469	605	952	1376
	12	9	17	28	49	68	112	160	248	333	429	675	976
	10	6	10	17	30	41	69	98	152	204	263	414	598
	8	3	6	11	19	26	43	62	96	129	166	261	378
	6	2	4	7	13	18	30	43	67	90	116	184	265
	4	1	3	5	9	12	21	30	46	62	80	126	183
	3	1	2	4	6	9	15	22	34	45	58	92	133
	2	1	1	3	5	7	12	18	28	38	49	77	111
	1	1	1	2	4	6	10	14	23	30	39	62	90
XHH, XHHW, XHHW-2, ZW	14	8	14	24	42	57	94	135	209	280	361	568	822
	12	6	11	18	32	44	72	103	160	215	277	436	631
	10	4	8	13	24	32	54	77	119	160	206	325	470
	8	2	4	7	13	18	30	43	66	89	115	181	261
	6	1	3	5	10	13	22	32	49	66	85	134	193
	4	1	2	4	7	9	16	23	35	48	61	97	140
	3	1	1	3	6	8	13	19	30	40	52	82	118
	2	1	1	3	5	7	11	16	25	34	44	69	99
XHH, XHHW, XHHW-2	1	1	1	1	3	5	8	12	19	25	32	51	74
	1/0	1	1	1	3	4	7	10	16	21	27	43	62
	2/0	0	1	1	2	3	6	8	13	17	22	36	52
	3/0	0	1	1	1	3	5	7	11	14	19	30	43
	4/0	0	1	1	1	2	4	6	9	12	15	24	35
	250	0	0	1	1	1	3	5	7	10	13	20	29
	300	0	0	1	1	1	3	4	6	8	11	17	25
	350	0	0	1	1	1	2	3	5	7	9	15	22
	400	0	0	0	1	1	1	3	5	6	8	13	19
	500	0	0	0	1	1	1	2	4	5	7	11	16
	600	0	0	0	1	1	1	1	3	4	5	9	13
	700	0	0	0	0	1	1	1	3	4	5	8	11
	750	0	0	0	0	1	1	1	2	3	4	7	11

* Types RHH, RHW, AND RHW-2 without outer covering.

See Ugly's page 134 for Trade Size / Metric Designator conversion.

MAXIMUM NUMBER OF CONDUCTORS IN *RIGID PVC CONDUIT, SCHEDULE 80*

Type Letters	Cond. Size AWG/kcmil	Trade Sizes In Inches											
		1/2	3/4	1	1 1/4	1 1/2	2	2 1/2	3	3 1/2	4	5	6
RHH, RHW, RHW-2	14	3	5	9	17	23	39	56	88	118	153	243	349
	12	2	4	7	14	19	32	46	73	98	127	202	290
	10	1	3	6	11	15	26	37	59	79	103	163	234
	8	1	1	3	6	8	13	19	31	41	54	85	122
	6	1	1	2	4	6	11	16	24	33	43	68	98
	4	1	1	1	3	5	8	12	19	26	33	53	77
	3	0	1	1	3	3	7	11	17	23	29	47	67
	2	0	1	1	3	4	6	9	14	20	25	41	58
	1	0	1	1	2	3	4	6	9	13	17	27	38
	1/0	0	0	1	1	1	3	5	8	11	15	23	33
	2/0	0	0	1	1	1	3	4	7	10	13	20	29
	3/0	0	0	1	1	1	3	4	6	8	11	17	25
	4/0	0	0	0	1	1	2	3	5	7	9	15	21
	250	0	0	0	1	1	1	2	4	5	7	11	16
	300	0	0	0	1	1	1	2	3	5	6	10	14
	350	0	0	0	1	1	1	1	3	4	5	9	13
	400	0	0	0	0	1	1	1	3	3	4	8	12
	500	0	0	0	0	1	1	1	2	3	4	7	10
	600	0	0	0	0	0	1	1	1	3	3	6	8
	700	0	0	0	0	0	1	1	1	2	3	5	7
	750	0	0	0	0	0	1	1	1	2	3	5	7
TW	14	6	11	20	35	49	82	118	185	250	324	514	736
	12	5	9	15	27	38	63	91	142	192	248	394	565
	10	3	6	11	20	28	47	67	106	143	185	294	421
	8	1	3	6	11	15	26	37	59	79	103	163	234
RHH*, RHW*, RHW-2*, THHW, THW, THW-2	14	4	8	13	23	32	55	79	123	166	215	341	490
RHH*, RHW*, RHW-2*, THHW, THW	12	3	6	10	19	26	44	63	99	133	173	274	394
	10	2	5	8	15	20	34	49	77	104	135	214	307
RHH*, RHW*, RHW-2*, THHW, THW, THW-2	8	1	3	5	9	12	20	29	46	62	81	128	184
RHH*, RHW*, RHW-2*, TW, THW, THHW, THW-2	6	1	1	3	7	9	16	22	35	48	62	98	141
	4	1	1	3	5	7	12	17	26	35	46	73	105
	3	1	1	2	4	6	10	14	22	30	39	63	90
	2	1	1	1	3	5	8	12	19	26	33	53	77
	1	0	1	1	2	3	6	8	13	18	23	37	54
	1/0	0	1	1	1	3	5	7	11	15	20	32	46
	2/0	0	1	1	1	2	4	6	10	13	17	27	39
	3/0	0	0	1	1	1	3	5	8	11	14	23	33
	4/0	0	0	1	1	1	3	4	7	9	12	19	27
	250	0	0	0	1	1	2	3	5	7	9	15	22
	300	0	0	0	1	1	1	3	5	6	8	13	19
	350	0	0	0	1	1	1	2	4	6	7	12	17
	400	0	0	0	1	1	1	2	4	5	7	11	15
	500	0	0	0	0	1	1	1	3	4	5	9	13
	600	0	0	0	0	1	1	1	2	3	4	7	10
	700	0	0	0	0	1	1	1	2	3	4	6	9
	750	0	0	0	0	0	1	1	1	3	3	6	8
THHN, THWN, THWN-2	14	9	17	28	51	70	118	170	265	358	464	736	1055
	12	6	12	20	37	51	86	124	193	261	338	537	770
	10	4	7	13	23	32	54	78	122	164	213	338	485
	8	2	4	7	13	18	31	45	70	95	123	195	279
	6	1	3	5	9	13	22	32	51	68	89	141	202
	4	1	1	3	6	8	14	20	31	42	54	86	124
	3	1	1	3	5	7	12	17	26	35	46	73	105
	2	1	1	2	4	6	10	14	22	30	39	61	88
	1	0	1	1	3	4	7	10	16	22	29	45	65

MAXIMUM NUMBER OF CONDUCTORS IN *RIGID PVC CONDUIT, SCHEDULE 80*

Type Letters	Cond. Size AWG/kcmil	Trade Sizes In Inches											
		1/2	3/4	1	1-1/4	1-1/2	2	2-1/2	3	3-1/2	4	5	6
THHN, THWN, THWN-2	1/0	0	1	1	2	3	6	9	14	18	24	38	55
	2/0	0	1	1	1	3	5	7	11	15	20	32	46
	3/0	0	1	1	1	2	4	6	9	13	17	26	38
	4/0	0	0	1	1	1	3	5	8	10	14	22	31
	250	0	0	1	1	1	3	4	6	8	11	18	25
	300	0	0	0	1	1	2	3	5	7	9	15	22
	350	0	0	0	1	1	1	3	5	6	8	13	19
	400	0	0	0	1	1	1	3	4	6	7	12	17
	500	0	0	0	1	1	1	2	3	5	6	10	14
	600	0	0	0	0	1	1	1	3	4	5	8	12
	700	0	0	0	0	1	1	1	2	3	4	7	10
	750	0	0	0	0	1	1	1	2	3	3	7	9
FEP, FEPB, PFA, PFAH, TFE	14	8	16	27	49	68	115	164	257	347	450	714	1024
	12	6	12	20	36	50	84	120	188	253	328	521	747
	10	4	8	14	26	36	60	86	135	182	235	374	536
	8	2	5	8	15	20	34	49	77	104	135	214	307
	6	1	3	6	10	14	24	35	55	74	96	152	218
	4	1	2	4	7	10	17	24	38	52	67	106	153
	3	1	1	3	6	8	14	20	32	43	56	89	127
	2	1	1	3	5	7	12	17	26	35	46	73	105
PFA, PFAH, TFE	1	1	1	1	3	5	8	11	18	25	32	51	73
PFA, PFAH, TFE, Z	1/0	0	1	1	3	4	7	10	15	20	27	42	61
	2/0	0	1	1	2	3	5	8	12	17	22	35	50
	3/0	0	1	1	1	2	4	6	10	14	18	29	41
	4/0	0	0	1	1	1	4	5	8	11	15	24	34
Z	14	10	19	33	59	82	138	198	310	418	542	860	1233
	12	7	14	23	42	58	98	141	220	297	385	610	875
	10	4	8	14	26	36	60	86	135	182	235	374	536
	8	3	5	9	16	22	38	54	85	115	149	236	339
	6	2	4	6	11	16	26	38	60	81	104	166	238
	4	1	2	4	8	11	18	26	41	55	72	114	164
	3	1	1	3	5	8	13	19	30	40	52	83	119
	2	1	1	2	5	6	11	16	25	33	43	69	99
	1	0	1	2	2	4	9	13	20	27	35	56	80
XHH, XHHW, XHHW-2, ZW	14	6	11	20	35	49	82	118	185	250	324	514	736
	12	5	9	15	27	38	63	91	142	192	248	394	565
	10	3	6	11	20	28	47	67	106	143	185	294	421
	8	1	3	6	11	15	26	37	59	79	103	163	234
	6	1	2	4	8	11	19	28	43	59	76	121	173
	4	1	1	3	6	8	14	20	31	42	55	87	125
	3	1	1	3	5	7	12	17	26	36	47	74	106
	2	1	1	2	4	6	10	14	22	30	39	62	89
XHH, XHHW, XHHW-2	1	0	1	1	3	4	7	10	16	22	29	46	66
	1/0	0	1	1	2	3	6	9	14	19	24	39	56
	2/0	0	1	1	1	3	5	7	11	16	20	32	46
	3/0	0	1	1	1	2	4	6	9	13	17	27	38
	4/0	0	0	1	1	1	3	5	8	11	14	22	32
	250	0	0	1	1	1	3	4	6	9	11	18	26
	300	0	0	1	1	1	2	3	5	7	10	15	22
	350	0	0	0	1	1	1	3	5	6	8	14	20
	400	0	0	0	1	1	1	3	4	6	7	12	17
	500	0	0	0	1	1	1	2	3	5	6	10	14
	600	0	0	0	0	1	1	1	3	4	5	8	11
	700	0	0	0	0	1	1	1	2	3	4	7	10
	750	0	0	0	0	1	1	1	2	3	3	6	9

* Types RHH, RHW, AND RHW-2 without outer covering.

See Ugly's page 134 for Trade Size / Metric Designator conversion.

Type Letters	Cond. Size AWG/kcmil	Trade Sizes In Inches											
		1/2	3/4	1	1 1/4	1 1/2	2	2 1/2	3	3 1/2	4	5	6
RHH, RHW, RHW-2	14	4	7	12	21	28	46	66	102	136	176	276	398
	12	3	6	10	17	23	38	55	85	113	146	229	330
	10	3	5	8	14	19	31	44	68	91	118	185	267
	8	1	2	4	7	10	16	23	36	48	61	97	139
	6	1	1	3	6	8	13	18	29	38	49	77	112
	4	1	1	2	4	6	10	14	22	30	38	60	87
	3	1	1	2	4	5	9	12	19	26	34	53	76
	2	1	1	1	3	4	7	11	17	23	29	46	66
	1	0	1	1	1	3	5	7	11	15	19	30	44
	1/0	0	1	1	1	2	4	6	10	13	17	26	38
	2/0	0	1	1	1	2	4	5	8	11	14	23	33
	3/0	0	0	1	1	1	3	4	7	10	12	20	28
	4/0	0	0	1	1	1	3	3	6	8	11	17	24
	250	0	0	0	1	1	1	3	4	6	8	13	18
	300	0	0	0	1	1	1	2	4	5	7	11	16
	350	0	0	0	1	1	1	2	4	5	6	10	15
	400	0	0	0	1	1	1	1	3	4	6	9	13
	500	0	0	0	0	1	1	1	3	4	5	8	11
	600	0	0	0	0	1	1	1	2	3	4	6	9
	700	0	0	0	0	1	1	1	1	3	4	6	8
	750	0	0	0	0	0	1	1	1	3	3	5	8
TW	14	9	15	25	44	59	98	140	216	288	370	581	839
	12	7	12	19	33	45	75	107	165	221	284	446	644
	10	5	9	14	25	34	56	80	123	164	212	332	480
	8	3	5	8	14	19	31	44	68	91	118	185	267
RHH*, RHW*, RHW-2*, THHN, THW, THW-2	14	6	10	17	29	39	65	93	143	191	246	387	558
RHH*, RHW*, RHW-2*, THHN, THW	12	5	8	13	23	32	52	75	115	154	198	311	448
	10	3	6	10	18	25	41	58	90	120	154	242	350
RHH*, RHW*, RHW-2*, THHN, THW, THW-2	8	1	4	6	11	15	24	35	54	72	92	145	209
RHH*, RHW*, RHW-2*, TW, THW, THHW, THW-2	6	1	3	5	8	11	18	27	41	55	71	111	160
	4	1	1	3	6	8	14	20	31	41	53	83	120
	3	1	1	3	5	7	12	17	26	35	45	71	103
	2	1	1	2	4	6	10	14	22	30	38	60	87
	1	1	1	1	3	4	7	10	15	21	27	42	61
	1/0	0	1	1	2	3	6	8	13	18	23	36	52
	2/0	0	1	1	2	2	5	7	11	15	19	31	44
	3/0	0	1	1	1	2	4	6	9	13	16	26	37
	4/0	0	0	1	1	1	3	5	8	10	14	21	31
	250	0	0	1	1	1	2	3	6	8	11	17	25
	300	0	0	1	1	1	2	3	5	7	9	15	22
	350	0	0	0	1	1	1	3	5	6	8	13	19
	400	0	0	0	1	1	1	3	4	6	7	12	17
	500	0	0	0	1	1	1	2	3	5	6	10	14
	600	0	0	0	1	1	1	1	3	4	5	8	12
	700	0	0	0	0	1	1	1	2	3	4	7	10
	750	0	0	0	0	1	1	1	2	3	4	7	10
THHN, THWN, THWN-2	14	13	22	36	63	85	140	200	309	412	531	833	1202
	12	9	16	26	46	62	102	146	225	301	387	608	877
	10	6	10	17	29	39	64	92	142	189	244	383	552
	8	3	6	9	16	22	37	53	82	109	140	221	318
	6	2	4	7	12	16	27	38	59	79	101	159	230
	4	1	2	4	7	10	16	23	36	48	62	98	141
	3	1	1	3	6	8	14	20	31	41	53	83	120
	2	1	1	3	5	7	11	17	26	34	44	70	100
	1	1	1	1	4	5	8	12	19	25	33	51	74

MAXIMUM NUMBER OF CONDUCTORS IN *RIGID METAL CONDUIT*

Type Letters	Cond. Size AWG/kcmil	Trade Sizes In Inches											
		1/2	3/4	1	1 1/4	1 1/2	2	2 1/2	3	3 1/2	4	5	6
THHN, THWN, THWN-2	1/0	1	1	1	3	4	7	10	16	21	27	43	63
	2/0	0	1	1	2	3	6	8	13	18	23	36	52
	3/0	0	1	1	1	3	5	7	11	15	19	30	43
	4/0	0	1	1	1	2	4	6	9	12	16	25	36
	250	0	0	1	1	1	3	5	7	10	13	20	29
	300	0	0	1	1	1	3	4	6	8	11	17	25
	350	0	0	1	1	1	2	3	5	7	10	15	22
	400	0	0	1	1	1	2	3	5	7	8	13	20
	500	0	0	0	1	1	1	2	4	5	7	11	16
	600	0	0	0	1	1	1	1	3	4	6	9	13
	700	0	0	0	1	1	1	1	3	4	5	8	11
	750	0	0	0	0	1	1	1	3	4	5	7	11
FEP, FEPB, PFA, PFAH, TFE	14	12	22	35	61	83	136	194	300	400	515	808	1166
	12	9	16	26	44	60	99	142	219	292	376	590	851
	10	6	11	18	32	43	71	102	157	209	269	423	610
	8	3	6	10	18	25	41	58	90	120	154	242	350
	6	2	4	7	13	17	29	41	64	85	110	172	249
	4	1	3	5	9	12	20	29	44	59	77	120	174
	3	1	2	4	7	10	17	24	37	50	64	100	145
	2	1	1	3	6	8	14	20	31	41	53	83	120
PFA, PFAH, TFE	1	1	1	1	2	4	6	9	14	21	28	57	83
PFA, PFAH, TFE, Z	1/0	1	1	1	3	5	8	11	18	24	30	48	69
	2/0	1	1	1	3	4	6	9	14	19	25	40	57
	3/0	0	1	1	2	3	5	8	12	16	21	33	47
	4/0	0	1	1	1	2	4	6	10	13	17	27	39
Z	14	15	26	42	73	100	164	234	361	482	621	974	1405
	12	10	18	30	52	71	116	166	256	342	440	691	997
	10	6	11	18	32	43	71	102	157	209	269	423	610
	8	4	7	11	20	27	45	64	99	132	170	267	386
	6	3	5	8	14	19	31	45	69	93	120	188	271
	4	1	3	5	9	13	22	31	48	64	82	129	186
	3	1	2	4	7	9	16	22	35	47	60	94	136
	2	1	1	3	6	8	13	19	29	39	50	78	113
	1	1	1	2	5	6	10	15	23	31	41	63	92
XHH, XHHW, XHHW-2, ZW	14	9	15	25	44	59	98	140	216	288	370	581	839
	12	7	12	19	33	45	75	107	165	221	284	446	644
	10	5	9	14	25	34	56	80	123	164	212	332	480
	8	3	5	8	14	19	31	44	68	91	118	185	267
	6	1	3	6	10	14	23	33	51	68	87	137	197
	4	1	2	4	7	10	16	24	37	49	63	99	143
	3	1	1	3	6	8	14	20	31	41	53	84	121
	2	1	1	3	5	7	12	17	26	35	45	70	101
	1	1	1	1	4	5	9	12	19	26	33	52	76
XHH, XHHW, XHHW-2	1/0	1	1	1	3	4	7	10	16	22	28	44	64
	2/0	0	1	1	2	3	6	9	13	18	23	37	53
	3/0	0	1	1	1	3	5	7	11	15	19	30	44
	4/0	0	1	1	1	2	4	6	9	12	16	25	36
	250	0	0	1	1	1	3	5	7	10	13	20	30
	300	0	0	1	1	1	3	4	6	9	11	18	25
	350	0	0	1	1	1	2	3	6	7	10	15	22
	400	0	0	1	1	1	2	3	5	7	9	14	20
	500	0	0	0	1	1	1	2	4	5	7	11	16
	600	0	0	0	1	1	1	1	3	4	6	9	13
	700	0	0	0	1	1	1	1	3	4	5	8	11
	750	0	0	0	0	1	1	1	3	4	5	7	11

* Types RHH, RHW, AND RHW-2 without outer covering.

See Ugly's page 134 for Trade Size / Metric Designator conversion.

MAXIMUM NUMBER OF CONDUCTORS IN *FLEXIBLE METAL CONDUIT*

Type Letters	Cond. Size AWG/kcmil	Trade Sizes In Inches									
		1/2	3/4	1	1 1/4	1 1/2	2	2 1/2	3	3 1/2	4
RHH, RHW, RHW-2	14	4	7	11	17	25	44	67	96	131	171
	12	3	6	9	14	21	37	55	80	109	142
	10	3	5	7	11	17	30	45	64	88	115
	8	1	2	4	6	9	15	23	34	46	60
	6	1	1	3	5	7	12	19	27	37	48
	4	1	1	2	4	5	10	14	21	29	37
	3	1	1	1	3	5	8	13	18	25	33
	2	1	1	1	3	4	7	11	16	22	28
	1	0	1	1	1	2	5	7	10	14	19
	1/0	0	1	1	1	2	4	6	9	12	16
	2/0	0	1	1	1	1	3	5	8	11	14
	3/0	0	0	1	1	1	3	5	7	9	12
	4/0	0	0	1	1	1	2	4	6	8	10
	250	0	0	0	1	1	1	3	4	6	8
	300	0	0	0	1	1	1	2	4	5	7
	350	0	0	0	1	1	1	2	3	5	6
	400	0	0	0	0	1	1	1	3	4	6
	500	0	0	0	0	1	1	1	3	4	5
	600	0	0	0	0	1	1	1	2	3	4
	700	0	0	0	0	0	1	1	1	3	3
	750	0	0	0	0	0	1	1	1	2	3
TW	14	9	15	23	36	53	94	141	203	277	361
	12	7	11	18	28	41	72	108	156	212	277
	10	5	8	13	21	30	54	81	116	158	207
	8	3	5	7	11	17	30	45	64	88	115
RHH*, RHW*, RHW-2*, THHW, THW, THW-2	14	6	10	15	24	35	62	94	135	184	240
RHH*, RHW*, RHW-2*, THHW, THW	12	5	8	12	19	28	50	75	108	148	193
	10	4	6	10	15	22	39	59	85	115	151
RHH*, RHW*, RHW-2*, THHW, THW, THW-2	8	1	4	6	9	13	23	35	51	69	90
RHH*, RHW*, RHW-2*, TW, THW, THHW, THW-2	6	1	3	4	7	10	18	27	39	53	69
	4	1	1	3	5	7	13	20	29	39	51
	3	1	1	3	4	6	11	17	25	34	44
	2	1	1	2	4	5	10	14	21	29	37
	1	1	1	1	2	4	7	10	15	20	26
	1/0	0	1	1	1	3	6	9	12	17	22
	2/0	0	1	1	1	3	5	7	10	14	19
	3/0	0	1	1	1	2	4	6	9	12	16
	4/0	0	0	1	1	1	3	5	7	10	13
	250	0	0	1	1	1	3	4	6	8	11
	300	0	0	1	1	1	2	3	5	7	9
	350	0	0	0	1	1	1	3	4	6	8
	400	0	0	0	1	1	1	3	4	6	7
	500	0	0	0	1	1	1	2	3	5	6
	600	0	0	0	0	1	1	1	3	4	5
	700	0	0	0	0	1	1	1	2	3	4
	750	0	0	0	0	1	1	1	2	3	4
THHN, THWN, THWN-2	14	13	22	33	52	76	134	202	291	396	518
	12	9	16	24	38	56	98	147	212	289	378
	10	6	10	15	24	35	62	93	134	182	238
	8	3	6	9	14	20	35	53	77	105	137
	6	2	4	6	10	14	25	38	55	76	99
	4	1	2	4	6	9	16	24	34	46	61
	3	1	1	3	5	7	13	20	29	39	51
	2	1	1	3	4	6	11	17	24	33	43
	1	1	1	1	3	4	8	12	18	24	32

MAXIMUM NUMBER OF CONDUCTORS IN *FLEXIBLE METAL CONDUIT*

Type Letters	Cond. Size AWG/kcmil	Trade Sizes In Inches									
		½	¾	1	1¼	1½	2	2½	3	3½	4
THHN, THWN, THWN-2	1/0	1	1	1	2	4	7	10	15	20	27
	2/0	0	1	1	1	3	6	9	12	17	22
	3/0	0	1	1	1	2	5	7	10	14	18
	4/0	0	1	1	1	1	4	6	8	12	15
	250	0	0	1	1	1	3	5	7	9	12
	300	0	0	1	1	1	3	4	6	8	11
	350	0	0	1	1	1	2	3	5	7	9
	400	0	0	0	1	1	1	3	5	6	8
	500	0	0	0	0	1	1	1	4	5	7
	600	0	0	0	0	1	1	1	3	4	5
	700	0	0	0	0	0	1	1	3	4	5
	750	0	0	0	0	0	1	1	2	3	4
FEP, FEPB, PFA, PFAH, TFE	14	12	21	32	51	74	130	196	282	385	502
	12	9	15	24	37	54	95	143	206	281	367
	10	6	11	17	26	39	68	103	148	201	263
	8	4	6	10	15	22	39	59	85	115	151
	6	2	4	7	11	16	28	42	60	82	107
	4	1	3	5	7	11	19	29	42	57	75
	3	1	2	4	6	9	16	24	35	48	62
	2	1	1	3	5	7	13	20	29	39	51
PFA, PFAH, TFE	1	1	1	2	3	5	9	14	20	27	36
PFA, PFAH, TFE, Z	1/0	1	1	1	3	4	8	11	17	23	30
	2/0	1	1	1	2	3	6	9	14	19	24
	3/0	0	1	1	1	3	5	8	11	15	20
	4/0	0	1	1	1	2	4	6	9	13	16
Z	14	15	25	39	61	89	157	236	340	463	605
	12	11	18	28	43	63	111	168	241	329	429
	10	6	11	17	26	39	68	103	148	201	263
	8	4	7	11	17	24	43	65	93	127	166
	6	3	5	7	12	17	30	45	65	89	117
	4	1	3	5	8	12	21	31	45	61	80
	3	1	2	4	6	8	15	23	33	45	58
	2	1	1	3	5	7	12	19	27	37	49
	1	1	1	2	4	6	10	15	22	30	39
XHH, XHHW, XHHW-2, ZW	14	9	15	23	36	53	94	141	203	277	361
	12	7	11	18	28	41	72	108	156	212	277
	10	5	8	13	21	30	54	81	116	158	207
	8	3	5	7	11	17	30	45	64	88	115
	6	1	3	5	8	12	22	33	48	65	85
	4	1	2	4	6	9	16	24	34	47	61
	3	1	1	3	5	7	13	20	29	40	52
	2	1	1	3	4	6	11	17	24	33	44
XHH, XHHW, XHHW-2	1	1	1	1	3	5	8	13	18	25	32
	1/0	1	1	1	2	4	7	10	15	21	27
	2/0	0	1	1	2	3	6	9	13	17	23
	3/0	0	1	1	1	3	5	7	10	14	19
	4/0	0	1	1	1	2	4	6	9	12	15
	250	0	0	1	1	1	3	5	7	10	13
	300	0	0	1	1	1	3	4	6	8	11
	350	0	0	1	1	1	2	3	5	7	9
	400	0	0	0	1	1	1	3	5	6	8
	500	0	0	0	1	1	1	3	4	5	7
	600	0	0	0	0	1	1	1	3	4	5
	700	0	0	0	0	1	1	1	3	4	5
	750	0	0	0	0	0	1	1	2	3	4

* Types RHH, RHW, AND RHW-2 without outer covering.

See Ugly's page 134 for Trade Size / Metric Designator conversion.

MAXIMUM NUMBER OF CONDUCTORS IN *LIQUIDTIGHT FLEXIBLE METAL CONDUIT*

Type Letters	Cond. Size AWG/kcmil	Trade Sizes In Inches									
		1/2	3/4	1	1 1/4	1 1/2	2	2 1/2	3	3 1/2	4
RHH, RHW, RHW-2	14	4	7	12	21	27	44	66	102	133	173
	12	3	6	10	17	22	36	55	84	110	144
	10	3	5	8	14	18	29	44	68	89	116
	8	1	2	4	7	9	15	23	36	46	61
	6	1	1	3	6	7	12	18	28	37	48
	4	1	1	2	4	5	9	14	22	29	38
	3	1	1	1	4	4	8	13	19	25	33
	2	1	1	1	3	4	7	11	17	22	29
	1	0	1	1	1	3	5	7	11	14	19
	1/0	0	1	1	1	3	4	6	10	13	16
	2/0	0	1	1	1	1	3	5	8	11	14
	3/0	0	0	1	1	1	3	4	7	9	12
	4/0	0	0	1	1	1	2	4	6	8	10
	250	0	0	0	1	1	1	3	4	6	8
	300	0	0	0	1	1	1	2	4	5	7
	350	0	0	0	1	1	1	2	3	5	6
	400	0	0	0	1	1	1	1	3	4	6
	500	0	0	0	1	1	1	1	3	4	5
	600	0	0	0	0	1	1	1	2	3	4
	700	0	0	0	0	0	1	1	1	3	3
	750	0	0	0	0	0	1	1	1	2	3
TW	14	9	15	25	44	57	93	140	215	280	365
	12	7	12	19	33	43	71	108	165	215	280
	10	5	9	14	25	32	53	80	123	160	209
	8	3	5	8	14	18	29	44	68	89	116
RHH*, RHW*, RHW-2*, THHW, THW, THW-2	14	6	10	16	29	38	62	93	143	186	243
RHH*, RHW*, RHW-2*, THHW, THW	12	5	8	13	23	30	50	75	115	149	195
	10	3	6	10	18	23	39	58	89	117	152
RHH*, RHW*, RHW-2*, THHW, THW, THW-2	8	1	4	6	11	14	23	35	53	70	91
RHH*, RHW*, RHW-2*, TW, THW, THHW, THW-2	6	1	3	5	8	11	18	27	41	53	70
	4	1	1	3	6	8	13	20	30	40	52
	3	1	1	3	5	7	11	17	26	34	44
	2	1	1	2	4	6	9	14	22	29	38
	1	1	1	1	3	4	7	10	15	20	26
	1/0	0	1	1	2	3	6	8	13	17	23
	2/0	0	1	1	2	3	5	7	11	15	19
	3/0	0	1	1	1	2	4	6	9	12	16
	4/0	0	0	1	1	1	3	5	8	10	13
	250	0	0	1	1	1	3	4	6	8	11
	300	0	0	1	1	1	2	3	5	7	9
	350	0	0	0	1	1	1	3	5	6	8
	400	0	0	0	1	1	1	3	4	6	7
	500	0	0	0	1	1	1	2	3	5	6
	600	0	0	0	1	1	1	1	3	4	5
	700	0	0	0	0	1	1	1	3	3	4
	750	0	0	0	0	1	1	1	2	3	4
THHN, THWN, THWN-2	14	13	22	36	63	81	133	201	308	401	523
	12	9	16	26	46	59	97	146	225	292	381
	10	6	10	16	29	37	61	92	141	184	240
	8	3	6	9	16	21	35	53	81	106	138
	6	2	4	7	12	15	25	38	59	76	100
	4	1	2	4	7	9	15	23	36	47	61
	3	1	1	3	6	8	13	20	30	40	52
	2	1	1	3	5	7	11	17	26	33	44
	1	1	1	1	4	5	8	12	19	25	32

MAXIMUM NUMBER OF CONDUCTORS IN *LIQUIDTIGHT FLEXIBLE METAL CONDUIT*

Type Letters	Cond. Size AWG/kcmil	Trade Sizes In Inches										
		1/2	3/4	1	1 1/4	1 1/2	2	2 1/2	3	3 1/2	4
THHN, THWN, THWN-2	1/0	1	1	1	3	4	7	10	16	21	27
	2/0	0	1	1	2	3	6	8	13	17	23
	3/0	0	1	1	1	3	5	7	11	14	19
	4/0	0	1	1	1	2	4	6	9	12	15
	250	0	0	1	1	1	3	5	7	10	12
	300	0	0	1	1	1	3	4	6	8	11
	350	0	0	1	1	1	3	3	6	7	9
	400	0	0	0	1	1	2	3	5	6	8
	500	0	0	0	1	1	1	3	5	6	7
	600	0	0	0	1	1	1	2	4	5	6
	700	0	0	0	1	1	1	1	3	4	5
	750	0	0	0	0	1	1	1	3	4	5
FEP, FEPB, PFA, PFAH, TFE	14	12	21	35	61	79	129	195	299	389	507
	12	9	15	25	44	57	94	142	218	284	370
	10	6	11	18	32	41	68	102	156	203	266
	8	3	6	10	18	23	39	58	89	117	152
	6	2	4	7	13	17	27	41	64	83	108
	4	1	3	5	9	12	19	29	44	58	75
	3	1	2	4	7	10	16	24	37	48	63
	2	1	1	3	6	8	13	20	30	40	52
PFA, PFAH, TFE	1	1	1	2	4	5	9	14	21	28	36
PFA, PFAH, TFE, Z	1/0	1	1	1	3	4	7	11	18	23	30
	2/0	1	1	1	3	4	6	9	14	19	25
	3/0	0	1	1	2	3	5	8	12	16	20
	4/0	0	1	1	1	2	4	6	10	13	17
Z	14	20	26	42	73	95	156	235	360	469	611
	12	14	18	30	52	67	111	167	255	332	434
	10	8	11	18	32	41	68	102	156	203	266
	8	5	7	11	20	26	43	64	99	129	168
	6	4	5	8	14	18	30	45	69	90	118
	4	2	3	5	9	12	20	31	48	62	81
	3	2	2	4	7	9	15	23	35	45	59
	2	1	1	3	6	7	12	19	29	38	49
	1	1	1	2	5	6	10	15	23	30	40
XHH, XHHW, XHHW-2, ZW	14	9	15	25	44	57	93	140	215	280	365
	12	7	12	19	33	43	71	108	165	215	280
	10	5	9	14	25	32	53	80	123	160	209
	8	3	5	8	14	18	29	44	68	89	116
	6	1	3	6	10	13	22	33	50	66	86
	4	1	2	4	7	9	16	24	36	48	62
	3	1	1	3	6	8	13	20	31	40	52
	2	1	1	3	5	7	11	17	26	34	44
	1	1	1	1	4	5	8	12	19	25	33
XHH, XHHW, XHHW-2	1/0	1	1	1	3	4	7	10	16	21	28
	2/0	0	1	1	2	3	6	9	13	17	23
	3/0	0	1	1	1	3	5	7	11	14	19
	4/0	0	1	1	1	2	4	6	9	12	16
	250	0	0	1	1	1	3	5	7	10	13
	300	0	0	1	1	1	3	4	6	8	11
	350	0	0	1	1	1	2	3	5	7	10
	400	0	0	0	1	1	1	3	5	6	8
	500	0	0	0	1	1	1	3	4	5	7
	600	0	0	0	1	1	1	2	3	4	6
	700	0	0	0	1	1	1	1	3	4	5
	750	0	0	0	0	1	1	1	3	3	5

* Types RHH, RHW, AND RHW-2 without outer covering.

See Ugly's page 134 for Trade Size / Metric Designator conversion.

Reprinted with permission from NFPA 70-2008, the *National Electrical Code®*, Copyright 2007, National Fire Protection Association, Quincy, MA 02269. This reprinted material is not the referenced subject which is represented only by the Standard in its entirety.

DIMENSIONS OF INSULATED CONDUCTORS & FIXTURE WIRES

TYPE	SIZE	APPROX. AREA SQ. IN.
RFH-2	18	0.0145
FFH-2	16	0.0172
RHW-2, RHH	14	0.0293
RHW	12	0.0353
	10	0.0437
	8	0.0835
	6	0.1041
	4	0.1333
	3	0.1521
	2	0.1750
	1	0.2660
	1/0	0.3039
	2/0	0.3505
	3/0	0.4072
	4/0	0.4754
	250	0.6291
	300	0.7088
	350	0.7870
	400	0.8626
	500	1.0082
	600	1.2135
	700	1.3561
	750	1.4272
	800	1.4957
	900	1.6377
	1000	1.7719
	1250	2.3479
	1500	2.6938
	1750	3.0357
	2000	3.3719
SF-2, SFF-2	18	0.0115
	16	0.0139
	14	0.0172
SF-1, SFF-1	18	0.0065
RFH-1, XF, XFF	18	0.0080
TF, TFF, XF, XFF	16	0.0109
TW, XF, XFF,	14	0.0139
THHW, THW, THW-2		
TW, THHW,	12	0.0181
THW, THW-2	10	0.0243
	8	0.0437
RHH*, RHW*, RHW-2*,	14	0.0209
RHH*, RHW*, RHW-2*,	12	0.0260
XF, XFF		

*Types RHH, RHW, and RHW-2 without outer covering

TYPE	SIZE	APPROX. AREA SQ. IN.
RHH*, RHW*, XF RHW-2*, XFF	10	0.0333
RHH*, RHW*, RHW-2*	8	0.0556
TW, THW	6	0.0726
THHW	4	0.0973
THW-2	3	0.1134
RHH*	2	0.1333
RHW*	1	0.1901
RHW-2*	1/0	0.2223
	2/0	0.2624
	3/0	0.3117
	4/0	0.3718
	250	0.4596
	300	0.5281
	350	0.5958
	400	0.6619
	500	0.7901
	600	0.9729
	700	1.1010
	750	1.1652
	800	1.2272
	900	1.3561
	1000	1.4784
	1250	1.8602
	1500	2.1695
	1750	2.4773
	2000	2.7818
TFN	18	0.0055
TFFN	16	0.0072
THHN	14	0.0097
THWN	12	0.0133
THWN-2	10	0.0211
	8	0.0366
	6	0.0507
	4	0.0824
	3	0.0973
	2	0.1158
	1	0.1562
	1/0	0.1855
	2/0	0.2223
	3/0	0.2679
	4/0	0.3237
	250	0.3970
	300	0.4608
	350	0.5242
	400	0.5863
	500	0.7073
	600	0.8676
	700	0.9887

Reprinted with permission from NFPA 70-2008, the *National Electrical Code*®, Copyright 2007, National Fire Protection Association, Quincy, MA 02269. This reprinted material is not the referenced subject which is represented only by the Standard in its entirety.

DIMENSIONS OF INSULATED CONDUCTORS & FIXTURE WIRES

TYPE	SIZE	APPROX. AREA SQ. IN.
THHN THWN THWN-2	750 800 900 1000	1.0496 1.1085 1.2311 1.3478
PF, PGFF, PGF, PFF, PTF, PAF, PTFF, PAFF	18 16	0.0058 0.0075
PF, PGFF, PGF, PFF, PTF, PAF, PTFF, PAFF TFE, FEP, PFA FEPB, PFAH	14	0.0100
TFE, FEP, PFA, FEPB, PFAH	12 10 8 6 4 3 2	0.0137 0.0191 0.0333 0.0468 0.0670 0.0804 0.0973
TFE, PFAH	1	0.1399
TFE, PFA, PFAH, Z	1/0 2/0 3/0 4/0	0.1676 0.2027 0.2463 0.3000
ZF, ZFF	18 16	0.0045 0.0061
Z, ZF, ZFF	14	0.0083
Z	12 10 8 6 4 3 2 1	0.0117 0.0191 0.0302 0.0430 0.0625 0.0855 0.1029 0.1269
XHHW, ZW XHHW-2 XHH	14 12 10 8 6 4 3 2	0.0139 0.0181 0.0243 0.0437 0.0590 0.0814 0.0962 0.1146
XHHW XHHW-2 XHH	1 1/0 2/0 3/0 4/0 250	0.1534 0.1825 0.2190 0.2642 0.3197 0.3904

TYPE	SIZE	APPROX. AREA SQ. IN.
XHHW XHHW-2 XHH	300 350 400 500 600 700 750 800 900 1000 1250 1500 1750 2000	0.4536 0.5166 0.5782 0.6984 0.8709 0.9923 1.0532 1.1122 1.2351 1.3519 1.7180 2.0157 2.3127 2.6073
KF-2 KFF-2	18 16 14 12 10	0.0031 0.0044 0.0064 0.0093 0.0139
KF-1 KFF-1	18 16 14 12 10	0.0026 0.0037 0.0055 0.0083 0.0127

*Types RHH, RHW, and RHW-2 without outer covering

See Ugly's page 132 - 138 for conversion of Square inches to mm².

COMPACT COPPER & ALUMINUM BUILDING WIRE NOMINAL DIMENSIONS* AND AREAS

Size AWG or kcmil	Bare Conductor		Types THW and THHW		Type THHN		Type XHHW		Size AWG or kcmil
	Number of Strands	Diam. Inches	Approx. Diam. Inches	Approx. Area Sq. In.	Approx. Diam. Inches	Approx. Area Sq. In.	Approx. Diam. Inches	Approx. Area Sq. Inches	
8	7	0.134	0.255	0.0510	—	—	0.224	0.0394	8
6	7	0.169	0.290	0.0660	0.240	0.0452	0.260	0.0530	6
4	7	0.213	0.335	0.0881	0.305	0.0730	0.305	0.0730	4
2	7	0.268	0.390	0.1194	0.360	0.1017	0.360	0.1017	2
1	19	0.299	0.465	0.1698	0.415	0.1352	0.415	0.1352	1
1/0	19	0.336	0.500	0.1963	0.450	0.1590	0.450	0.1590	1/0
2/0	19	0.376	0.545	0.2332	0.495	0.1924	0.490	0.1885	2/0
3/0	19	0.423	0.590	0.2733	0.540	0.2290	0.540	0.2290	3/0
4/0	19	0.475	0.645	0.3267	0.595	0.2780	0.590	0.2733	4/0
250	37	0.520	0.725	0.4128	0.670	0.3525	0.660	0.3421	250
300	37	0.570	0.775	0.4717	0.720	0.4071	0.715	0.4015	300
350	37	0.616	0.820	0.5281	0.770	0.4656	0.760	0.4536	350
400	37	0.659	0.865	0.5876	0.815	0.5216	0.800	0.5026	400
500	37	0.736	0.940	0.6939	0.885	0.6151	0.880	0.6082	500
600	61	0.813	1.050	0.8659	0.985	0.7620	0.980	0.7542	600
700	61	0.877	1.110	0.9676	1.050	0.8659	1.050	0.8659	700
750	61	0.908	1.150	1.0386	1.075	0.9076	1.090	0.9331	750
900	61	0.999	1.224	1.1766	1.194	1.1196	1.169	1.0733	900
1000	61	1.060	1.285	1.2968	1.255	1.2370	1.230	1.1882	1000

* Dimensions are from industry sources.

See Ugly's page 130 - 138 for metric conversions.

DIMENSIONS AND PERCENT AREA OF CONDUIT AND TUBING
(for the combinations of wires permitted in Table 1, Chapter 9, *NEC* ©)
(See Ugly's page 130 - 138 for metric conversion)

Trade Size Inches	Internal Diameter Inches	Total Area 100% Sq. in.	2 Wires 31% Sq. in.	Over 2 Wires 40% Sq. in.	1 Wire 53% Sq. in.	(NIPPLE) 60% Sq. in.
ELECTRICAL METALLIC TUBING (EMT)						
¹/₂	0.622	0.304	0.094	0.122	0.161	0.182
³/₄	0.824	0.533	0.165	0.213	0.283	0.320
1	1.049	0.864	0.268	0.346	0.458	0.519
1¹/₄	1.380	1.496	0.464	0.598	0.793	0.897
1¹/₂	1.610	2.036	0.631	0.814	1.079	1.221
2	2.067	3.356	1.040	1.342	1.778	2.013
2¹/₂	2.731	5.858	1.816	2.343	3.105	3.515
3	3.356	8.846	2.742	3.538	4.688	5.307
3¹/₂	3.834	11.545	3.579	4.618	6.119	6.927
4	4.334	14.753	4.573	5.901	7.819	8.852
ELECTRICAL NONMETALLIC TUBING (ENT)						
¹/₂	0.560	0.246	0.076	0.099	0.131	0.148
³/₄	0.760	0.454	0.141	0.181	0.240	0.272
1	1.000	0.785	0.243	0.314	0.416	0.471
1¹/₄	1.340	1.410	0.437	0.564	0.747	0.846
1¹/₂	1.570	1.936	0.600	0.774	1.026	1.162
2	2.020	3.205	0.993	1.282	1.699	1.923
2¹/₂	–	–	–	–	–	–
3	–	–	–	–	–	–
3¹/₂	–	–	–	–	–	–
4	–	–	–	–	–	–
FLEXIBLE METAL CONDUIT (FMC)						
³/₈	0.384	0.116	0.036	0.046	0.061	0.069
¹/₂	0.635	0.317	0.098	0.127	0.168	0.190
³/₄	0.824	0.533	0.165	0.213	0.283	0.320
1	1.020	0.817	0.253	0.327	0.433	0.490
1¹/₄	1.275	1.277	0.396	0.511	0.677	0.766
1¹/₂	1.538	1.858	0.576	0.743	0.985	1.115
2	2.040	3.269	1.013	1.307	1.732	1.961
2¹/₂	2.500	4.909	1.522	1.963	2.602	2.945
3	3.000	7.069	2.191	2.827	3.746	4.241
3¹/₂	3.500	9.621	2.983	3.848	5.099	5.773
4	4.000	12.566	3.896	5.027	6.660	7.540
INTERMEDIATE METAL CONDUIT (IMC)						
³/₈	–	–	–	–	–	–
¹/₂	0.660	0.342	0.106	0.137	0.181	0.205
³/₄	0.864	0.586	0.182	0.235	0.311	0.352
1	1.105	0.959	0.297	0.384	0.508	0.575
1¹/₄	1.448	1.647	0.510	0.659	0.873	0.988
1¹/₂	1.683	2.225	0.690	0.890	1.179	1.335
2	2.150	3.630	1.125	1.452	1.924	2.178
2¹/₂	2.557	5.135	1.592	2.054	2.722	3.081
3	3.176	7.922	2.456	3.169	4.199	4.753
3¹/₂	3.671	10.584	3.281	4.234	5.610	6.351
4	4.166	13.631	4.226	5.452	7.224	8.179

DIMENSIONS AND PERCENT AREA OF CONDUIT AND TUBING
(for the combinations of wires permitted in Table 1, Chapter 9, *NEC*®)
(See Ugly's page 130 - 138 for metric conversion)

Trade Size Inches	Internal Diameter Inches	Total Area 100% Sq. in.	2 Wires 31% Sq. in.	Over 2 Wires 40% Sq. in.	1 Wire 53% Sq. in.	(NIPPLE) 60% Sq. in.
LIQUIDTIGHT FLEXIBLE NONMETALLIC CONDUIT (TYPE LFNC-B*)						
³/₈	0.494	0.192	0.059	0.077	0.102	0.115
¹/₂	0.632	0.314	0.097	0.125	0.166	0.188
³/₄	0.830	0.541	0.168	0.216	0.287	0.325
1	1.054	0.873	0.270	0.349	0.462	0.524
1¹/₄	1.395	1.528	0.474	0.611	0.810	0.917
1¹/₂	1.588	1.981	0.614	0.792	1.050	1.188
2	2.033	3.246	1.006	1.298	1.720	1.948

* Corresponds to Section 356.2(2).

Trade Size Inches	Internal Diameter Inches	Total Area 100% Sq. in.	2 Wires 31% Sq. in.	Over 2 Wires 40% Sq. in.	1 Wire 53% Sq. in.	(NIPPLE) 60% Sq. in.
LIQUIDTIGHT FLEXIBLE NONMETALLIC CONDUIT (TYPE LFNC-A*)						
³/₈	0.495	0.192	0.060	0.077	0.102	0.115
¹/₂	0.630	0.312	0.097	0.125	0.165	0.187
³/₄	0.825	0.535	0.166	0.214	0.283	0.321
1	1.043	0.854	0.265	0.342	0.453	0.513
1¹/₄	1.383	1.502	0.466	0.601	0.796	0.901
1¹/₂	1.603	2.018	0.626	0.807	1.070	1.211
2	2.063	3.343	1.036	1.337	1.772	2.006

* Corresponds to Section 356.2(1).

Trade Size Inches	Internal Diameter Inches	Total Area 100% Sq. in.	2 Wires 31% Sq. in.	Over 2 Wires 40% Sq. in.	1 Wire 53% Sq. in.	(NIPPLE) 60% Sq. in.
LIQUIDTIGHT FLEXIBLE METAL CONDUIT (LFMC)						
³/₈	0.494	0.192	0.059	0.077	0.102	0.115
¹/₂	0.632	0.314	0.097	0.125	0.166	0.188
³/₄	0.830	0.541	0.168	0.216	0.287	0.325
1	1.054	0.873	0.270	0.349	0.462	0.524
1¹/₄	1.395	1.528	0.474	0.611	0.810	0.917
1¹/₂	1.588	1.981	0.614	0.792	1.050	1.188
2	2.033	3.246	1.006	1.298	1.720	1.948
2¹/₂	2.493	4.881	1.513	1.953	2.587	2.929
3	3.085	7.475	2.317	2.990	3.962	4.485
3¹/₂	3.520	9.731	3.017	3.893	5.158	5.839
4	4.020	12.692	3.935	5.077	6.727	7.615

Trade Size Inches	Internal Diameter Inches	Total Area 100% Sq. in.	2 Wires 31% Sq. in.	Over 2 Wires 40% Sq. in.	1 Wire 53% Sq. in.	(NIPPLE) 60% Sq. in.
RIGID METAL CONDUIT (RMC)						
³/₈	–	–	–	–	–	–
¹/₂	0.632	0.314	0.097	0.125	0.166	0.188
³/₄	0.836	0.549	0.170	0.220	0.291	0.329
1	1.063	0.887	0.275	0.355	0.470	0.532
1¹/₄	1.394	1.526	0.473	0.610	0.809	0.916
1¹/₂	1.624	2.071	0.642	0.829	1.098	1.243
2	2.083	3.408	1.056	1.363	1.806	2.045
2¹/₂	2.489	4.866	1.508	1.946	2.579	2.919
3	3.090	7.499	2.325	3.000	3.974	4.499
3¹/₂	3.570	10.010	3.103	4.004	5.305	6.006
4	4.050	12.882	3.994	5.153	6.828	7.729
5	5.073	20.212	6.266	8.085	10.713	12.127
6	6.093	29.158	9.039	11.663	15.454	17.495

DIMENSIONS AND PERCENT AREA OF CONDUIT AND TUBING
(for the combinations of wires permitted in Table 1, Chapter 9, *NEC* ©)
(See Ugly's page 130 - 138 for metric conversion)

Trade Size Inches	Internal Diameter Inches	Total Area 100% Sq. in.	2 Wires 31% Sq. in.	Over 2 Wires 40% Sq. in.	1 Wire 53% Sq. in.	(NIPPLE) 60% Sq. in.
RIGID PVC CONDUIT (PVC), SCHEDULE 80						
¹/₂	0.526	0.217	0.067	0.087	0.115	0.130
³/₄	0.722	0.409	0.127	0.164	0.217	0.246
1	0.936	0.688	0.213	0.275	0.365	0.413
1¹/₄	1.255	1.237	0.383	0.495	0.656	0.742
1¹/₂	1.476	1.711	0.530	0.684	0.907	1.027
2	1.913	2.874	0.891	1.150	1.523	1.725
2¹/₂	2.290	4.119	1.277	1.647	2.183	2.471
3	2.864	6.442	1.997	2.577	3.414	3.865
3¹/₂	3.326	8.688	2.693	3.475	4.605	5.213
4	3.786	11.258	3.490	4.503	5.967	6.755
5	4.768	17.855	5.535	7.142	9.463	10.713
6	5.709	25.598	7.935	10.239	13.567	15.359
RIGID PVC CONDUIT (PVC), SCHEDULE 40 & HDPE CONDUIT (HDPE)						
¹/₂	0.602	0.285	0.088	0.114	0.151	0.171
³/₄	0.804	0.508	0.157	0.203	0.269	0.305
1	1.029	0.832	0.258	0.333	0.441	0.499
1¹/₄	1.360	1.453	0.450	0.581	0.770	0.872
1¹/₂	1.590	1.986	0.616	0.794	1.052	1.191
2	2.047	3.291	1.020	1.316	1.744	1.975
2¹/₂	2.445	4.695	1.455	1.878	2.488	2.817
3	3.042	7.268	2.253	2.907	3.852	4.361
3¹/₂	3.521	9.737	3.018	3.895	5.161	5.842
4	3.998	12.554	3.892	5.022	6.654	7.532
5	5.016	19.761	6.126	7.904	10.473	11.856
6	6.031	28.567	8.856	11.427	15.141	17.140
TYPE A, RIGID PVC CONDUIT (PVC)						
¹/₂	0.700	0.385	0.119	0.154	0.204	0.231
³/₄	0.910	0.650	0.202	0.260	0.345	0.390
1	1.175	1.084	0.336	0.434	0.575	0.651
1¹/₄	1.500	1.767	0.548	0.707	0.937	1.060
1¹/₂	1.720	2.324	0.720	0.929	1.231	1.394
2	2.155	3.647	1.131	1.459	1.933	2.188
2¹/₂	2.635	5.453	1.690	2.181	2.890	3.272
3	3.230	8.194	2.540	3.278	4.343	4.916
3¹/₂	3.690	10.694	3.315	4.278	5.668	6.416
4	4.180	13.723	4.254	5.489	7.273	8.234
TYPE EB, PVC CONDUIT (PVC)						
2	2.221	3.874	1.201	1.550	2.053	2.325
2¹/₂	–	–	–	–	–	–
3	3.330	8.709	2.700	3.484	4.616	5.226
3¹/₂	3.804	11.365	3.523	4.546	6.023	6.819
4	4.289	14.448	4.479	5.779	7.657	8.669
5	5.316	22.195	6.881	8.878	11.763	13.317
6	6.336	31.530	9.774	12.612	16.711	18.918

THREAD DIMENSIONS AND TAP DRILL SIZES

COARSE THREAD SERIES

NOMINAL SIZE	THREADS PER IN.	TAP DRILL	CLEARANCE DRILL
5/64"	48	47	36
1/8"	40	38	29
6	32	36	25
8	32	29	16
10	24	25	13/64"
12	24	16	7/32"
1/4"	20	7	17/64"
5/16"	18	F	21/64"
3/8"	16	5/16"	25/64"
7/16"	14	U	29/64"
1/2"	13	27/64"	33/64"
9/16"	12	31/64"	37/64"
5/8"	11	17/32"	41/64"
3/4"	10	21/32"	49/64"
7/8"	9	49/64"	57/64"
1"	8	7/8"	1-1/64"
1-1/4"	7	1-7/64"	1-17/64"
1-3/8"	6	1-11/64"	1-19/64"
1-1/2"	6	1-19/64"	1-25/64"
2"	4-1/2	1-25/32"	2-1/32"

FINE THREAD SERIES

NOMINAL SIZE	THREADS PER IN.	TAP DRILL	CLEARANCE DRILL
0	80	3/64"	51
1	72	53	47
2	64	50	42
3	56	45	36
4	48	42	31
1/8"	44	37	29
6	40	33	25
8	36	29	16
10	32	21	13/64"
12	28	16	7/32"
1/4"	28	3	17/64"
5/16"	24	O	21/64"
3/8"	24	1	25/64"
7/16"	20	14	29/64"
1/2"	20	3	33/64"
9/16"	18	25/64"	37/64"
5/8"	18	29/64"	41/64"
3/4"	16	37/64"	49/64"
7/8"	14	11/16"	57/64"
1	14	13/16"	1-1/64"

HOLE SAW CHART *

TRADE SIZE	RIGID CONDUIT	E.M.T. CONDUIT	GREEN-FIELD	L.T. FLEX.	TRADE SIZE	RIGID CONDUIT	E.M.T. CONDUIT	GREEN-FIELD
1/2"	7/8"	3/4"	1"	1-1/8"	2-1/2"	3"	2-7/8"	2-7/8"
3/4"	1-1/8"	1"	1-1/8"	1-1/4"	3"	3-5/8"	3-1/2"	3-5/8"
1"	1-3/8"	1-1/4"	1-1/2"	1-1/2"	3-1/2"	4-1/8"	4"	4-1/8"
1-1/4"	1-3/4"	1-5/8"	1-3/4"	1-3/4"	4"	4-5/8"	4-1/2"	4-5/8"
1-1/2"	2"	1-7/8"	2"	1-7/8"	5"	5-3/4"		
2"	2-1/2"	2-1/8"	2-1/2"	2-3/4"	6"	6-3/4"		

NOTE: For oil type push button station, use size 1-7/32" knock-out punch.

* For connectors, (male connectors and adapters), use Rigid Table.

METAL BOXES

BOX DIMENSION, INCHES TRADE SIZE OR TYPE	MIN. CU. IN. CAPACITY	MAXIMUM NUMBER OF CONDUCTORS						
		NO. 18	NO. 16	NO. 14	NO. 12	NO. 10	NO. 8	NO. 6
4 x 1-1/4 ROUND OR OCTAGONAL	12.5	8	7	6	5	5	4	2
4 x 1-1/2 ROUND OR OCTAGONAL	15.5	10	8	7	6	6	5	3
4 x 2-1/8 ROUND OR OCTAGONAL	21.5	14	12	10	9	8	7	4
4 x 1-1/4 SQUARE	18.0	12	10	9	8	7	6	3
4 x 1-1/2 SQUARE	21.0	14	12	10	9	8	7	4
4 x 2-1/8 SQUARE	30.3	20	17	15	13	12	10	6
4-11/16 x 1-1/4 SQUARE	25.5	17	14	12	11	10	8	5
4-11/16 x 1-1/2 SQUARE	29.5	19	16	14	13	11	9	5
4-11/16 x 2-1/8 SQUARE	42.0	28	24	21	18	16	14	8
3 x 2 x 1-1/2 DEVICE	7.5	5	4	3	3	3	2	1
3 x 2 x 2 DEVICE	10.0	6	5	5	4	4	3	2
3 x 2 x 2-1/4 DEVICE	10.5	7	6	5	4	4	3	2
3 x 2 x 2-1/2 DEVICE	12.5	8	7	6	5	5	4	2
3 x 2 x 2-3/4 DEVICE	14.0	9	8	7	6	5	4	2
3 x 2 x 3-1/2 DEVICE	18.0	12	10	9	8	7	6	3
4 x 2-1/8 x 1-1/2 DEVICE	10.3	6	5	5	4	4	3	2
4 x 2-1/8 x 1-7/8 DEVICE	13.0	8	7	6	5	5	4	2
4 x 2-1/8 x 2-1/8 DEVICE	14.5	9	8	7	6	5	4	2
3-3/4 x 2 x 2-1/2 MASONRY BOX/GANG	14.0	9	8	7	6	5	4	2
3-3/4 x 2 x 3-1/2 MASONRY BOX/GANG	21.0	14	12	10	9	8	7	4
FS-MINIMUM INTERNAL DEPTH 1-3/4 SINGLE COVER/GANG	13.5	9	7	6	6	5	4	2
FD-MINIMUM INTERNAL DEPTH 2-3/8 SINGLE COVER/GANG	18.0	12	10	9	8	7	6	3
FS-MINIMUM INTERNAL DEPTH 1-3/4 MULTIPLE COVER/GANG	18.0	12	10	9	8	7	6	3
FD-MINIMUM INTERNAL DEPTH 2-3/8 MULTIPLE COVER/GANG	24.0	16	13	12	10	9	8	4

MINIMUM COVER REQUIREMENTS 0 - 600 VOLTS, NOMINAL

Cover is defined as the distance between the top surface of direct burial cable, conduit, or other raceways and the finished surface.

WIRING METHOD	MINIMUM BURIAL (INCHES)
DIRECT BURIAL CABLES	24
RIGID METAL CONDUIT	6*
INTERMEDIATE METAL CONDUIT	6*
RIGID NONMETALLIC CONDUIT (APPROVED FOR DIRECT BURIAL WITHOUT CONCRETE ENCASEMENT)	18*

*For most locations, for complete details, refer to National Electrical Code® Table 300-5 for exceptions such as highways, dwellings, airports, driveways, parking lots, etc. See Ugly's page 130 - 138 for metric conversions.

VOLUME REQUIRED PER CONDUCTOR

SIZE OF CONDUCTOR	FREE SPACE WITHIN BOX FOR EACH CONDUCTOR
No. 18	1.5 CUBIC INCHES
No. 16	1.75 CUBIC INCHES
No. 14	2 CUBIC INCHES
No. 12	2.25 CUBIC INCHES
No. 10	2.5 CUBIC INCHES
No. 8	3 CUBIC INCHES
No. 6	5 CUBIC INCHES

For complete details see NEC 314.16B.   See Ugly's page 130 - 138 for metric conversions.

SPACINGS FOR CONDUCTOR SUPPORTS

AWG or Circular-Mil Size of Wire	Support of Conductors in Vertical Raceways	CONDUCTORS Aluminum or Copper-Clad Aluminum	Copper
18 AWG through 8 AWG	Not greater than	100 feet	100 feet
6 AWG through 1/0 AWG	Not greater than	200 feet	100 feet
2/0 AWG through 4/0 AWG	Not greater than	180 feet	80 feet
Over 4/0 AWG through 350 kcmil	Not greater than	135 feet	60 feet
Over 350 kcmil through 500 kcmil	Not greater than	120 feet	50 feet
Over 500 kcmil through 750 kcmil	Not greater than	95 feet	40 feet
Over 750 kcmil	Not greater than	85 feet	35 feet

For SI units: one foot = 0.3048 meter.   See Ugly's page 130 - 138 for metric conversions.

MINIMUM DEPTH OF CLEAR WORKING SPACE IN FRONT OF ELECTRICAL EQUIPMENT

NOMINAL VOLTAGE TO GROUND	CONDITIONS		
	1	2	3
	Minimum clear distance (feet)		
0 - 150	3	3	3
151 - 600	3	3-1/2	4
601 - 2500	3	4	5
2501 - 9000	4	5	6
9001 - 25,000	5	6	9
25,001 - 75 kV	6	8	10
Above 75 kV	8	10	12

NOTES:

1. For SI units, 1 ft. = 0.3048 m.
2. Where the conditions are as follows:
   Condition 1 – Exposed live parts on one side of the working space and no live or grounded parts on the other side of the working space, or exposed live parts on both sides of the working space that are effectively guarded by insulating materials.
   Condition 2 – Exposed live parts on one side of the working space and grounded parts on the other side of the working space. Concrete, brick, or tile walls shall be considered as grounded.
   Condition 3 – Exposed live parts on both sides of the work space.

See Ugly's page 130 - 138 for metric conversion.

MINIMUM CLEARANCE OF LIVE PARTS

NOMINAL VOLTAGE RATING KV	IMPULSE WITHSTAND B.I.L. KV		*MINIMUM CLEARANCE OF LIVE PARTS, INCHES			
			PHASE-TO-PHASE		PHASE-TO-GROUND	
	INDOORS	OUTDOORS	INDOORS	OUTDOORS	INDOORS	OUTDOORS
2.4 - 4.16	60	95	4.5	7	3.0	6
7.2	75	95	5.5	7	4.0	6
13.8	95	110	7.5	12	5.0	7
14.4	110	110	9.0	12	6.5	7
23	125	150	10.5	15	7.5	10
34.5	150	150	12.5	15	9.5	10
	200	200	18.0	18	13.0	13
46		200		18		13
		250		21		17
69		250		21		17
		350		31		25
115		550		53		42
138		550		53		42
		650		63		50
161		650		63		50
		750		72		58
230		750		72		58
		900		89		71
		1050		105		83

For SI units: one inch = 25.4 millimeters

* The values given are the minimum clearance for rigid parts and bare conductors under favorable service conditions. They shall be increased for conductor movement or under unfavorable service conditions, or wherever space limitations permit. The selection of the associated impulse withstand voltage for a particular system voltage is determined by the characteristics of the surge protective equipment.

See Ugly's page 130 - 138 for metric conversion.

MINIMUM SIZE EQUIPMENT GROUNDING CONDUCTORS FOR GROUNDING RACEWAY AND EQUIPMENT

RATING OR SETTING OF AUTOMATIC OVERCURRENT DEVICE IN CIRCUIT AHEAD OF EQUIPMENT, CONDUIT, ETC., NOT EXCEEDING (AMPERES)	SIZE	
	COPPER	ALUMINUM OR COPPER-CLAD ALUMINUM*
15	14	12
20	12	10
30	10	8
40	10	8
60	10	8
100	8	6
200	6	4
300	4	2
400	3	1
500	2	1/0
600	1	2/0
800	1/0	3/0
1000	2/0	4/0
1200	3/0	250 kcmil
1600	4/0	350 kcmil
2000	250 kcmil	400 kcmil
2500	350 kcmil	600 kcmil
3000	400 kcmil	600 kcmil
4000	500 kcmil	800 kcmil
5000	700 kcmil	1200 kcmil
6000	800 kcmil	1200 kcmil

NOTE: Where necessary to comply with Section 250.4(A)(5) or 250.4(B)(4), the equipment grounding conductor shall be sized larger than given in this table.
* See installation restrictions in NEC 250.120.

Reprinted with permission from NFPA 70-2008, the *National Electrical Code*®, Copyright 2007, National Fire Protection Association, Quincy, MA 02269. This reprinted material is not the referenced subject which is represented only by the Standard in its entirety.

GROUNDING ELECTRODE CONDUCTOR FOR ALTERNATING-CURRENT SYSTEMS

SIZE OF LARGEST UNGROUNDED SERVICE-ENTRANCE CONDUCTOR OR EQUIVALENT AREA FOR PARALLEL CONDUCTORS*		SIZE OF GROUNDING ELECTRODE CONDUCTOR	
COPPER	ALUMINUM OR COPPER-CLAD ALUMINUM	COPPER	ALUMINUM OR COPPER-CLAD ALUMINUM**
2 OR SMALLER	1/0 OR SMALLER	8	6
1 OR 1/0	2/0 OR 3/0	6	4
2/0 OR 3/0	4/0 OR 250 kcmil	4	2
OVER 3/0 THRU 350kcmil	OVER 250 THRU THRU 500 kcmil	2	1/0
OVER 350 kcmil THRU 600 kcmil	OVER 500 kcmil THRU 900 kcmil	1/0	3/0
OVER 600 kcmil THRU 1100 kcmil	OVER 900 kcmil THRU 1750 kcmil	2/0	4/0
OVER 1100 kcmil	OVER 1750 kcmil	3/0	250 kcmil

NOTES:
1. Where multiple sets of service-entrance conductors are used as permit ted in Section 230.40, Exception No. 2, the equivalent size of the largest service-entrance conductor shall be determined by the largest sum of the areas of the corresponding conductors of each set.
2. Where there are no service-entrance conductors, the grounding electrode conductor size shall be determined by the equivalent size of the largest service-entrance conductor required for the load to be served.

   *This table also applies to the derived conductors of separately derived ac systems.

   **See installation restrictions in Section 250.64(a).

   FPN: See Section 250-24(c) for size of ac system conductor brought to service equipment.

GENERAL LIGHTING LOADS BY OCCUPANCY

TYPE OF OCCUPANCY	VOLT-AMPERES PER SQUARE FOOT
Armories & auditoriums	1
Banks	3 1/2[b]
Barber shops & beauty parlors	3
Churches	1
Clubs	2
Court rooms	2
Dwelling units[a]	3
Garages - commercial (storage)	1/2
Hospitals	2
Hotels & motels, including apartment houses without provision for cooking by tenants[a]	2
Industrial commercial (loft) buildings	2

TYPE OF OCCUPANCY	VOLT-AMPERES PER SQUARE FOOT
Lodge rooms	1½
Office buildings	3 1/2[b]
Restaurants	2
Schools	3
Stores	3
Warehouses (storage)	1/4
In any of the preceding occupancies except one-family dwellings & individual dwelling units of two-family & multi-family dwellings:	
Assembly halls & auditoriums	1
Halls, corridors, closets, stairways	1/2
Storage spaces	1/4

[a] See NEC 220.14(J)
[b] See NEC 220.14(K)

LIGHTING LOAD DEMAND FACTORS

Type of Occupancy	Portion of Lighting Load to Which Demand Factor Applies (Volt-Amperes)	Demand Factor (Percent)
Dwelling units	First 3000 or less at	100
	From 3001 to 120,000 at	35
	Remainder over 120,000 at	25
Hospitals*	First 50,000 or less at	40
	Remainder over 50,000 at	20
Hotels and motels, including apartment houses without provision for cooking by tenants*	First 20,000 or less at	50
	From 20,001 to 100,000 at	40
	Remainder over 100,000 at	30
Warehouses (Storage)	First 12,500 or less at	100
	Remainder over 12,500 at	50
All others	Total volt-amperes	100

* The demand factors of this table shall not apply to the computed load of feeders or services supplying areas in hospitals, hotels, and motels where the entire lighting is likely to be used at one time, as in operating rooms, ballrooms, or dining rooms.

DEMAND FACTORS FOR NONDWELLING RECEPTACLE LOADS

Portion of Receptacle Load to Which Demand Factor Applies (Volt-Amperes)	Demand Factor (Percent)
First 10 kVA or less at	100
Remainder over 10 kVA at	50

DEMAND FACTORS FOR HOUSEHOLD ELECTRIC CLOTHES DRYERS

Number of Dryers	Demand Factor (Percent)
1 - 4	100%
5	85%
6	75%
7	65%
8	60%
9	55%
10	50%
11	47%
12 - 23	47% minus 1% for each dryer exceeding 11
24 - 42	35% minus 0.5% for each dryer exceeding 23
43 and over	25%

DEMAND FACTORS FOR KITCHEN EQUIPMENT - OTHER THAN DWELLING UNIT(S)

Number of Units of Equipment	Demand Factor (Percent)
1	100
2	100
3	90
4	80
5	70
6 and over	65

<u>Note:</u> In no case shall the feeder or service calculated load be less than the sum of the largest two kitchen equipment loads.

DEMAND LOADS FOR HOUSEHOLD ELECTRIC RANGES, WALL-MOUNTED OVENS, COUNTER-MOUNTED COOKING UNITS, and OTHER HOUSEHOLD COOKING APPLIANCES over 1 3/4 kW RATING

(Column C to be used in all cases except as otherwise permitted in note 3)

| Number of Appliances | Demand Factor (Percent) (See Notes) | | Column C Maximum Demand (kW) (See Notes) (not over 12 kW Rating) |
	Column A (less than 3 1/2 kW Rating)	Column B (3 1/2 kW through 8 3/4 kW Rating)	
1	80	80	8
2	75	65	11
3	70	55	14
4	66	50	17
5	62	45	20
6	59	43	21
7	56	40	22
8	53	36	23
9	51	35	24
10	49	34	25
11	47	32	26
12	45	32	27
13	43	32	28
14	41	32	29
15	40	32	30
16	39	28	31
17	38	28	32
18	37	28	33
19	36	28	34
20	35	28	35
21	34	26	36
22	33	26	37
23	32	26	38
24	31	26	39
25	30	26	40
26 - 30	30	24	15 kW + 1 kW for each range
31 - 40	30	22	
41 - 50	30	20	25 kW + 3/4 kW for each range
51 - 60	30	18	
61 and over	30	16	

See Next page for Notes to this table

DEMAND LOADS FOR HOUSEHOLD ELECTRIC RANGES, WALL-MOUNTED OVENS, COUNTER-MOUNTED COOKING UNITS, and OTHER HOUSE-HOLD COOKING APPLIANCES over 1 3/4 kW RATING
NOTES

1. Over 12 kW through 27 kW ranges all of same rating. For ranges individually rated more than 12 kW but not more than 27 kW, the maximum demand in Column C shall be increased 5 percent for each additional kilowatt of rating or major fraction thereof by which the rating of individual ranges exceeds 12 kW.

2. Over 8¾ kW through 27 kW ranges of unequal ratings. For ranges individually rated more than 8¾ kW and of different ratings, but none exceeding 27 kW, an average value of rating shall be computed by adding together the ratings of all ranges to obtain the total connected load (using 12 kW for any range rated less than 12 kW) and dividing the total number of ranges. Then the maximum demand in Column C shall be increased 5 percent for each kilowatt or major fraction thereof by which this average value exceeds 12 kW.

3. Over 1¾ kW through 8¾ kW. In lieu of the method provided in Column C, it shall be permissible to add the nameplate ratings of all household cooking appliances rated more than 1¾ kW but not more than 8¾ kW and multiply the sum by the demand factors specified in Column A or B for the given number of appliances. Where the rating of cooking appliances falls under both Column A and Column B, the demand factors for each column shall be applied to the appliances for that column, and the results added together.

4. Branch-Circuit Load. It shall be permissible to compute the branch-circuit load for one range in accordance with Table 220.19. The branch-circuit load for one wall-mounted oven or one counter-mounted cooking unit shall be the nameplate rating of the appliance. The branch-circuit load for a counter-mounted cooking unit and not more than two wall-mounted ovens, all supplied from a single branch circuit and located in the same room, shall be computed by adding the nameplate rating of the individual appliances and treating this total as equivalent to one range.

5. This table also applies to household cooking appliances rated over 1¾ kW and used in instructional programs.

CALCULATING COST OF OPERATING
AN ELECTRICAL APPLIANCE

What is the monthly cost of operating a 240-volt 5-kilowatt (kW) Central electric heater that operates 12 hours per day, when the cost is 15 cents per kilowatt-hour (kWhr)?

Cost = Watts X Hours used X Rate per kWhr / 1000

5 kW = 5,000 Watts
Hours = 12 hours X 30 days = 360 hours per month

= 5,000 X 360 x .15 / 1,000
= 270,000 / 1,000 = **$270 Monthly cost**

The above example is for a resistive load. Air-conditioning loads are primarily inductive loads. However, if ampere and voltage values are known this method will give an approximate cost. Kilowatt-hour rates vary for different power companies, and for residential use, graduated rate scales are usually used (the more power used, the lower the rate). Commercial and industrial rates are generally based on kilowatt usage, maximum demand and power factor. Other costs are often added such as fuel cost adjustments.

CHANGING INCANDESCENT LAMP TO
ENERGY SAVING LAMP

A 100 watt incandescent lamp is to be replaced with a 26 watt energy saving lamp that has the same light output (lumens). If the cost per kilowatt-hour (kWhr) is 15 cents, how many hours would the new lamp need to operate to pay for itself?

Lamp cost is 3 dollars.   Energy saved is 74 watts.
Hours = Lamp cost X 1000 / Watts saved X kWhr

3 X 1,000 / 74 X .15 = 3,000 / 11.1 = 270.27 hours
The energy saving lamp will pay for itself with 270.27 hours of operation.

The comparative operating cost of these two lamps based on 270.27 hours is found by:
Cost = Watts X Hours used X Rate per kWhr / 1000
100-watt incandescent lamp = $4.05 for 270.27 hours of operation
26-watt energy saving lamp = $1.05 for 270.27 hours of operation

PARTIAL 2008 NEC CODE CHANGE SUMMARY

MULTI-WIRE BRANCH CIRCUITS NEC 210.4(B)
Multi-wire branch circuits shall have a disconnecting means that will simultaneously open all ungrounded (hot) conductors at the point of origination.

MULTI-WIRE BRANCH CIRCUITS NEC 210.4(D)
Multi-wire branch circuit ungrounded (hot) and grounded (neutral) conductors shall be grouped together by wire ties or other means in one location within the panelboard or other point of origination, unless grouping of conductors is obvious. NEC 210.4(D)(exception)

LUMINARIES (DISCONNECTING MEANS) NEC 410.130(G)(1)(2)(3)
Luminaries (lighting fixtures) installed in other than dwellings utilizing double ended lamps and that contain ballasts connected to multi-wire Branch circuits shall have an internal or external disconnecting means that will sinultaneously break all supply conductors to the ballast including the ungrounded (neutral) conductor.

GROUND-FAULT CIRCUIT INTERUPTER PROTECTION NEC 210.8(A)(2)(5)
Ground-fault interupter protection is required for **ALL** receptacles in **Dwelling unit** garages, accessory buildings and unfinished basement areas. The exceptions for appliances that were not readily accessible and dedicated branch circuits for a cord and plug connected appliances have been dropped. **GFCI** protection required for dwelling boat hoists outlets not exceeding 240 volts. NEC 210.8(C).

GROUND-FAULT CIRCUIT INTERUPTER PROTECTION NEC 210(A)(3)&(B)(4)
Ground-fault interupter protection is required for **ALL** Outdoor receptacles.

GROUND-FAULT CIRCUIT INTERUPTER PROTECTION NEC 422.511
Vending machines manufactured January 1, 2005 or later shall have Ground-Fault protection as an integral part of or within 12 inches of the attachment plug. Vending machines manufactured or remanufactured prior to January 1, 2005 shall be installed on GFCI protected outlet.

GROUND-FAULT CIRCUIT INTERUPTER PROTECTION NEC 422.52
(Electric drinking fountains) Electric drinking fountains shall be protected with ground-fault circuit interupter protection.

PARTIAL 2008 NEC CODE CHANGE SUMMARY
(continued)

ARC-FAULT CIRCUIT INTERUPTER PROTECTION NEC 210.12(B)
Arc-fault circuit interrupter protection is required for **ALL** 120-volt 15 and 20 ampere **Dwelling** unit branch circuits that supply outlets in family rooms, dining rooms, living rooms, parlors, libraries, dens, bedrooms, sunrooms, recreation rooms, closets, hallways and similar areas.

TAMPER-RESISTANT RECEPTACLES NEC 406.11
Tamper-resistant receptacles are required for all 125-volt 15 and 20-ampere receptacles required by NEC article 210.52 in **Dwelling units**.

GROUNDED CONDUCTORS NEC 210.19(A)(EXCEPTION 2)
215.2A(1)(EXCEPTION 2)
Grounded (neutral) conductors that are not connected to an overcurrent protective device that supplies continuous and/or non-continuous loads shall be permitted to be sized for 100% of the load.

SWITCHBOARDS AND PANELBOARDS (Field Markings) NEC 408.3(F)
Switchboards and Panelboards containing a Delta three-phase four wire system, where the midpoint of one phase is grounded shall be field marked: CAUTION ___PHASE HAS ___VOLT TO GROUND

PANELBOARDS (Overcurrent protection) NEC 408.36
A panelboard shall be protected by an overcurrent device having a rating that does not exceed that of the panelboard. The terms lighting and appliance and power Panelboards have been removed from this code section. The 42 circuit limitation has been removed from the general rule, but is referred to in the NEC 408.36(exception)(2) for Panelboards protected by two sets of overcurrent devices on the supply side of the panelboard.

GROUNDING BUILDINGS SUPPLIED BY A FEEDER OR BRANCH CIRCUIT
NEC 250.32(A)(B)
A separate building or structure supplied by a feeder or branch circuit shall have an Equipment grounding conductor sized in accordance with Table 250.122 run with the supply conductors and is to be connected to the building disconnecting means and an grounding electrode. The grounded (neutral) conductor is not to be used for any equipment grounding or connection to a

PARTIAL 2008 NEC CODE CHANGE SUMMARY

(continued)

grounding electrode. There is an exception for existing separate building for using the grounded (neutral) conductor for grounding purposes as allowed in the 2005 NEC. NEC 250.32(B)(exception)(1)(2)(3).

TEMPERATURE ADJUSTMENT FACTORS FOR CONDUITS EXPOSED TO SUNLIGHT ON OR ABOVE ROOFTOPS NEC TABLE 310.15B(2)(c)

A new NEC table for adding degrees of temperature to the ambient temperature to obtain the correct temperature correction factor for conduits exposed to sunlight on or above rooftops under various conditions.

NEW 2008 NEC ARTICLES

285 - Surge Protective Devices (SPDs) 1kV or less
355 - Reinforced thermosetting Conduit Type RTRC
522 - Control Systems for Permanent Amusement Attractions
626 - Electrified Truck Parking Spaces
708 - Critical Operations Power Systems (COPS)

FIELD TERMS VERSUS NEC TERMS

• BX	Armored cable (NEC 320)
• Romex	Non-metallic sheathed cable (NEC 334)
• Green field	Flexible metal conduit (MNEC 348)
• Thin wall	Electrical metallic tubing (NEC 358)
• Smurf tube	Electrical non-metallic tubing (NEC 362)
• 1900 box	4 inch square box (NEC 314)
• 333 box	Device box (NEC 314)
• EYS	Explosion proof seal off (NEC 500)
• Neutral**	Grounded conductor (NEC 200)**
• Ground wire	Equipment grounding conductor (NEC 250.118)
• Ground wire	Grounding electrode conductor (NEC 250.66)
• Hot, live	Ungrounded conductor

** Some systems do not have a neutral and the grounded conductor may be a phase conductor. (See NEC Article 100 neutral definition)

ELECTRICAL SYMBOLS

WALL	CEILING		SWITCH OUTLETS	
─◯	◯	OUTLET	S	SINGLE POLE SWITCH
─Ⓓ	Ⓓ	DROP CORD	S_2	DOUBLE POLE SWITCH
─Ⓕ	Ⓕ	FAN OUTLET	S_3	THREE WAY SWITCH
─Ⓙ	Ⓙ	JUNCTION BOX	S_4	FOUR WAY SWITCH
─Ⓛ	Ⓛ	LAMP HOLDER	S_D	AUTOMATIC DOOR SWITCH
─Ⓛ PS	Ⓛ PS	LAMP HOLDER WITH PULL SWITCH	S_E	ELECTROLIER SWITCH
─Ⓢ	Ⓢ	PULL SWITCH	S_P	SWITCH AND PILOT LAMP
─Ⓥ	Ⓥ	VAPOR DISCHARGE SWITCH	S_K	KEY OPERATED SWITCH
─Ⓧ	Ⓧ	EXIT OUTLET	S_{CB}	CIRCUIT BREAKER
─Ⓒ	Ⓒ	CLOCK OUTLET	S_{WCB}	WEATHER PROOF CIRCUIT BREAKER
─Ⓑ	Ⓑ	BLANKED OUTLET	S_{MC}	MOMENTARY CONTACT SWITCH

DUPLEX CONVENIENCE OUTLET

S_{RC} REMOTE CONTROL SWITCH

SINGLE, TRIPLEX, ETC. ₁,₃

S_{WP} WEATHER PROOF SWITCH

RANGE OUTLET

S_F FUSED SWITCH

SWITCH AND CONVENIENCE OUTLET ₛ

S_{WPF} WEATHER PROOF FUSED SWITCH

SPECIAL PURPOSE OUTLET

▆ LIGHTING PANEL

FLOOR OUTLET

▨ POWER PANEL

ELECTRICAL SYMBOLS

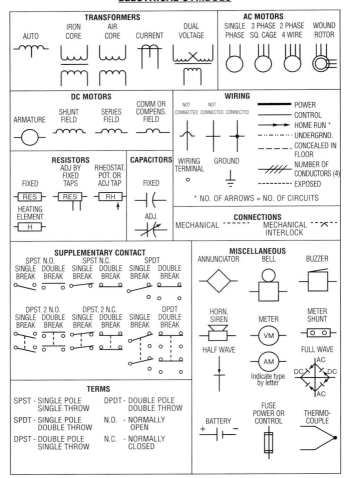

TRANSFORMERS

AUTO | IRON CORE | AIR CORE | CURRENT | DUAL VOLTAGE

AC MOTORS

SINGLE PHASE | 3 PHASE SQ. CAGE | 2 PHASE 4 WIRE | WOUND ROTOR

DC MOTORS

ARMATURE | SHUNT FIELD | SERIES FIELD | COMM OR COMPENS. FIELD

WIRING

NOT CONNECTED | NOT CONNECTED | CONNECTED

WIRING TERMINAL | GROUND

━━━━ POWER
──── CONTROL
──→ HOME RUN *
─·─·─· UNDERGRND.
───── CONCEALED IN FLOOR
─///─ NUMBER OF CONDUCTORS (4)
------ EXPOSED

* NO. OF ARROWS = NO. OF CIRCUITS

RESISTORS

FIXED | ADJ BY FIXED TAPS | RHEOSTAT. POT. OR ADJ TAP

HEATING ELEMENT

─[RES]─ | ─[RES]─ | ─[RH]─

─[H]─

CAPACITORS

FIXED

ADJ.

CONNECTIONS

MECHANICAL - - - - - MECHANICAL INTERLOCK ─×─

SUPPLEMENTARY CONTACT

SPST N.O. | SPST N.C. | SPDT
SINGLE BREAK | DOUBLE BREAK | SINGLE BREAK | DOUBLE BREAK | SINGLE BREAK | DOUBLE BREAK

DPST, 2 N.O. | DPST, 2 N.C. | DPDT
SINGLE BREAK | DOUBLE BREAK | SINGLE BREAK | DOUBLE BREAK | SINGLE BREAK | DOUBLE BREAK

MISCELLANEOUS

ANNUNCIATOR | BELL | BUZZER

HORN, SIREN | METER | METER SHUNT

HALF WAVE | VM | ─o o─ FULL WAVE

AM Indicate type by letter

AC DC ──╳── DC AC

BATTERY | FUSE POWER OR CONTROL | THERMO-COUPLE

TERMS

SPST - SINGLE POLE SINGLE THROW
SPDT - SINGLE POLE DOUBLE THROW
DPST - DOUBLE POLE SINGLE THROW
DPDT - DOUBLE POLE DOUBLE THROW
N.O. - NORMALLY OPEN
N.C. - NORMALLY CLOSED

ELECTRICAL SYMBOLS

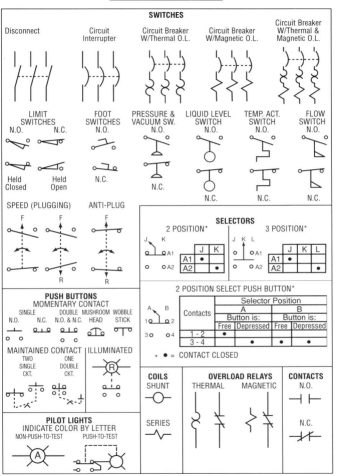

SWITCHES

| Disconnect | Circuit Interrupter | Circuit Breaker W/Thermal O.L. | Circuit Breaker W/Magnetic O.L. | Circuit Breaker W/Thermal & Magnetic O.L. |

| LIMIT SWITCHES N.O. N.C. | FOOT SWITCHES N.O. | PRESSURE & VACUUM SW. N.O. | LIQUID LEVEL SWITCH N.O. | TEMP. ACT. SWITCH N.O. | FLOW SWITCH N.O. |

Held Closed   Held Open

N.C.

N.C.   N.C.   N.C.   N.C.

SPEED (PLUGGING)   ANTI-PLUG

F   F   F

R   R   R

SELECTORS

2 POSITION*   3 POSITION*

	J	K
A1	•	
A2		•

	J	K	L
A1	•		
A2			•

2 POSITION SELECT PUSH BUTTON*

	Selector Position			
Contacts	A		B	
	Button is:		Button is:	
	Free	Depressed	Free	Depressed
1 - 2	•			
3 - 4		•	•	

* • = CONTACT CLOSED

PUSH BUTTONS
MOMENTARY CONTACT
SINGLE   DOUBLE   MUSHROOM WOBBLE
N.O.   N.C.   N.O. & N.C. HEAD   STICK

MAINTAINED CONTACT | ILLUMINATED
TWO   ONE
SINGLE   DOUBLE
CKT.   CKT.

COILS	OVERLOAD RELAYS		CONTACTS
SHUNT	THERMAL	MAGNETIC	N.O.
SERIES			N.C.

PILOT LIGHTS
INDICATE COLOR BY LETTER
NON-PUSH-TO-TEST   PUSH-TO-TEST

NOTE: N.O. = Normally Open;   N.C. = Normally Closed

WIRING DIAGRAMS FOR NEMA CONFIGURATIONS

2 Pole, 2 Wire Non-Grounding 125V

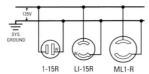

1-15R LI-15R ML1-R

2 Pole, 2 Wire Non-Grounding 250V

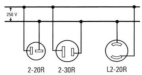

2-20R 2-30R L2-20R

2 Pole, 3 Wire Grounding 125V

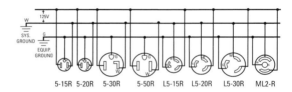

5-15R 5-20R 5-30R 5-50R L5-15R L5-20R L5-30R ML2-R

2 Pole, 3 Wire Grounding 250V

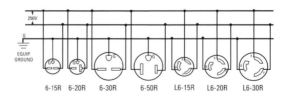

6-15R 6-20R 6-30R 6-50R L6-15R L6-20R L6-30R

2 Pole, 3 Wire Grounding 277V AC

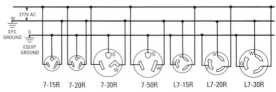

7-15R 7-20R 7-30R 7-50R L7-15R L7-20R L7-30R

Courtesy of

COOPER Wiring Devices
The New Power in Wiring Devices

WIRING DIAGRAMS FOR NEMA CONFIGURATIONS

**2 Pole, 3 Wire
Grounding
480V AC**

L8-20R L8-30R

**3 Pole, 3 Wire
Non-Grounding
125/250V**

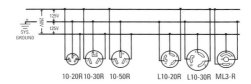

10-20R 10-30R 10-50R   L10-20R L10-30R ML3-R

**3 Pole, 3 Wire
Non-Grounding
3ø 250V**

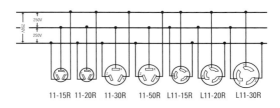

11-15R 11-20R 11-30R 11-50R L11-15R L11-20R L11-30R

**3 Pole, 4 Wire
Grounding
125/250V**

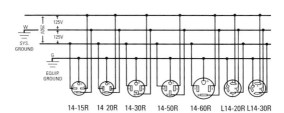

14-15R 14 20R 14-30R 14-50R 14-60R L14-20R L14-30R

WIRING DIAGRAMS FOR NEMA CONFIGURATIONS

3 Pole, 4 Wire Grounding 3ø 250V

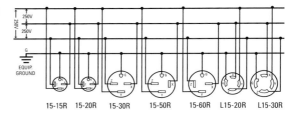

15-15R   15-20R   15-30R   15-50R   15-60R   L15-20R   L15-30R

3 Pole, 4 Wire Grounding 3ø 480V

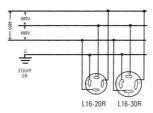

L16-20R   L16-30R

3 Pole, 4 Wire Grounding 3ø 600V

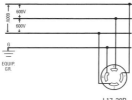

L17-30R

WIRING DIAGRAMS FOR NEMA CONFIGURATIONS

**4 Pole, 4 Wire
Non-Grounding
3ø 120/208V**

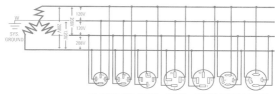

18-15R 18-20R 18-30R 18-50R 18-60R L18-20R L18-30R

**4 Pole, 4 Wire
Non-Grounding
3ø 277/480V**

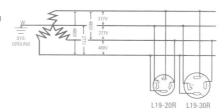

L19-20R L19-30R

**4 Pole, 4 Wire
Non-Grounding
3ø 347/600V**

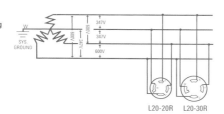

L20-20R L20-30R

Courtesy of

COOPER Wiring Devices
The New Power in Wiring Devices

WIRING DIAGRAMS FOR NEMA CONFIGURATIONS

4 Pole, 5 Wire Grounding 3ø 120/208V

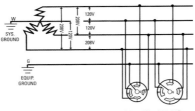

L21-20R   L21-30R

4 Pole, 5 Wire Grounding 3ø 277/480V

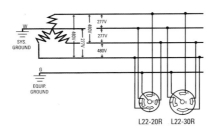

L22-20R   L22-30R

4 Pole, 5 Wire Grounding 3ø 347/600V

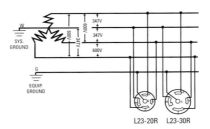

L23-20R   L23-30R

NEMA ENCLOSURE TYPES
NON-HAZARDOUS LOCATIONS

The purpose of this document is to provide general information on the definitions of NEMA Enclosure Types to architects, engineers, installers, inspectors and other interested parties. [For more detailed and complete information, NEMA Standards Publication 250-2003, "Enclosures for Electrical Equipment (1000 Volts Maximum)" should be consulted.

In **Non-Hazardous Locations**, the specific enclosure Types, their applications, and the environmental conditions they are designed to protect against, when completely and properly installed, are as follows:

Type 1 - Enclosures constructed for indoor use to provide a degree of protection to personnel against incidental contact with the enclosed equipment and to provide a degree of protection against falling dirt.

Type 2 - Enclosures constructed for indoor use to provide a degree of protection to personnel against incidental contact with the enclosed equipment, to provide a degree of protection against falling dirt, and to provide a degree of protection against dripping and light splashing of liquids.

Type 3 - Enclosures constructed for either indoor or outdoor use to provide a degree of protection to personnel against incidental contact with the enclosed equipment; to provide a degree of protection against falling dirt, rain, sleet, snow, and windblown dust; and that will be undamaged by the external formation of ice on the enclosure.

Type 3R - Enclosures constructed for either indoor or outdoor use to provide a degree of protection to personnel against incidental contact with the enclosed equipment; to provide a degree of protection against falling dirt, rain, sleet, and snow; and that will be undamaged by the external formation of ice on the enclosure.

Type 3S - Enclosures constructed for either indoor or outdoor use to provide a degree of protection to personnel against incidental contact with the enclosed equipment; to provide a degree of protection against falling dirt, rain, sleet, snow, and windblown dust; and in which the external mechanism(s) remain operable when ice laden.

Type 4 - Enclosures constructed for either indoor or outdoor use to provide a degree of protection to personnel against incidental contact with the enclosed equipment; to provide a degree of protection against falling dirt, rain, sleet, snow, windblown dust, splashing water, and hose-directed water; and that will be undamaged by the external formation of ice on the enclosure.

Type 4X - Enclosures constructed for either indoor or outdoor use to provide a degree of protection to personnel against incidental contact with the enclosed equipment; to provide a degree of protection against falling dirt, rain, sleet, snow, windblown dust, splashing water, hose-directed water, and corrosion; and that will be undamaged by the external formation of ice on the enclosure.

Type 5 - Enclosures constructed for indoor use to provide a degree of protection to personnel against incidental contact with the enclosed equipment; to provide a degree of protection against falling dirt; against settling airborne dust, lint, fibers, and flyings; and to provide a degree of protection against dripping and light splashing of liquids.

Type 6 - Enclosures constructed for either indoor or outdoor use to provide a degree of protection to personnel against incidental contact with the enclosed equipment; to provide a degree of protection against falling dirt; against hose-directed water and the entry of water during occasional temporary submersion at a limited depth; and that will be undamaged by the external formation of ice on the enclosure.

Type 6P - Enclosures constructed for either indoor or outdoor use to provide a degree of protection to personnel against incidental contact with the enclosed equipment; to provide a degree of protection against falling dirt; against hose-directed water and the entry of water during prolonged submersion at a limited depth; and that will be undamaged by the external formation of ice on the enclosure.

Type 12 - Enclosures constructed (without knockouts) for indoor use to provide a degree of protection to personnel against incidental contact with the enclosed equipment; to provide a degree of protection against falling dirt; against circulating dust, lint, fibers, and flyings; and against dripping and light splashing of liquids.

NEMA ENCLOSURE TYPES *(cont'd)*
NON-HAZARDOUS LOCATIONS

Type 12K - Enclosures constructed (with knockouts) for indoor use to provide a degree of protection to personnel against incidental contact with the enclosed equipment; to provide a degree of protection against falling dirt; against circulating dust, lint, fibers, and flyings; and against dripping and light splashing of liquids.

Type 13 - Enclosures constructed for indoor use to provide a degree of protection to personnel against incidental contact with the enclosed equipment; to provide a degree of protection against falling dirt; against circulating dust, lint, fibers, and flyings; and against the spraying, splashing, and seepage of water, oil, and noncorrosive coolants.

HAZARDOUS LOCATIONS

In Hazardous Locations, when completely and properly installed and maintained, Type 7 and Type 10 enclosures are designed to contain an internal explosion without causing an external hazard. Type 8 enclosures are designed to prevent combustion through the use of oil-immersed equipment. Type 9 enclosures are designed to prevent the ignition of combustible dust.

Type 7 - Enclosures constructed for indoor use in hazardous locations classified as Class I, Division 1, Groups A, B, C or D as defined in NFPA 70.

Type 8 - Enclosures constructed for either indoor or outdoor use in hazardous locations classified as Class I, Division 1, Groups A, B, C or D as defined in NFPA 70.

Type 9 - Enclosures constructed for indoor use in hazardous conditions classified as Class II, Division 1, Groups E, F or G as defined in NFPA 70.

Type 10 - Enclosures constructed to meet the requirements of the Mine Safety and Health Administration, 30 CFR, Part 18.

(from NEMA 250-2003 - reprinted with permission)

U.S. WEIGHTS AND MEASURES

LINEAR MEASURE

			1	INCH	=	2.540	CENTIMETERS
12	INCHES	=	1	FOOT	=	3.048	DECIMETERS
3	FEET	=	1	YARD	=	9.144	DECIMETERS
5.5	YARDS	=	1	ROD	=	5.029	METERS
40	RODS	=	1	FURLONG	=	2.018	HECTOMETERS
8	FURLONGS	=	1	MILE	=	1.609	KILOMETERS

MILE MEASUREMENTS

1	STATUTE MILE	=	5,280	FEET
1	SCOTS MILE	=	5,952	FEET
1	IRISH MILE	=	6,720	FEET
1	RUSSIAN VERST	=	3,504	FEET
1	ITALIAN MILE	=	4,401	FEET
1	SPANISH MILE	=	15,084	FEET

OTHER LINEAR MEASUREMENTS

1 HAND	=	4	INCHES	1 LINK	=	7.92	INCHES
1 SPAN	=	9	INCHES	1 FATHOM	=	6	FEET
1 CHAIN	=	22	YARDS	1 FURLONG	=	10	CHAINS
				1 CABLE	=	608	FEET

SQUARE MEASURE

144	SQUARE INCHES	=	1	SQUARE FOOT
9	SQUARE FEET	=	1	SQUARE YARD
30 1/4	SQUARE YARDS	=	1	SQUARE ROD
40	RODS	=	1	ROOD
4	ROODS	=	1	ACRE
640	ACRES	=	1	SQUARE MILE
1	SQUARE MILE	=	1	SECTION
36	SECTIONS	=	1	TOWNSHIP

CUBIC OR SOLID MEASURE

1	CU. FOOT	=	1728	CU. INCHES
1	CU. YARD	=	27	CU. FEET
1	CU. FOOT	=	7.48	GALLONS
1	GALLON (WATER)	=	8.34	LBS.
1	GALLON (U.S.)	=	231	CU. INCHES OF WATER
1	GALLON (IMPERIAL)	=	277 1/4	CU. INCHES OF WATER

U.S. WEIGHTS AND MEASURES

LIQUID MEASUREMENTS

1	PINT	=	4	GILLS
1	QUART	=	2	PINTS
1	GALLON	=	4	QUARTS
1	FIRKIN	=	9	GALLONS (ALE OR BEER)
1	BARREL	=	42	GALLONS (PETROLEUM OR CRUDE OIL)

DRY MEASURE

1	QUART	=	2	PINTS
1	PECK	=	8	QUARTS
1	BUSHEL	=	4	PECKS

WEIGHT MEASUREMENT (MASS)

A. AVOIRDUPOIS WEIGHT:

1	OUNCE	=	16	DRAMS
1	POUND	=	16	OUNCES
1	HUNDREDWEIGHT	=	100	POUNDS
1	TON	=	2,000	POUNDS

B. TROY WEIGHT:

1	CARAT	=	3.17	GRAINS
1	PENNYWEIGHT	=	20	GRAINS
1	OUNCE	=	20	PENNYWEIGHTS
1	POUND	=	12	OUNCES
1	LONG HUNDRED-WEIGHT	=	112	POUNDS
1	LONG TON	=	20	LONG HUNDREDWEIGHTS
		=	2240	POUNDS

C. APOTHECARIES WEIGHT:

1	SCRUPLE	=	20	GRAINS	=	1.296	GRAMS
1	DRAM	=	3	SCRUPLES	=	3.888	GRAMS
1	OUNCE	=	8	DRAMS	=	31.1035	GRAMS
1	POUND	=	12	OUNCES	=	373.2420	GRAMS

D. KITCHEN WEIGHTS AND MEASURES:

1	U.S. PINT	=	16	FL. OUNCES
1	STANDARD CUP	=	8	FL. OUNCES
1	TABLESPOON	=	0.5	FL. OUNCES (15 CU. CMS.)
1	TEASPOON	=	0.16	FL. OUNCES (5 CU. CMS.)

METRIC SYSTEM

PREFIXES:

A. MEGA	=	1,000,000		E. DECI	=	0.1
B. KILO	=	1,000		F. CENTI	=	0.01
C. HECTO	=	100		G. MILLI	=	0.001
D. DEKA	=	10		H. MICRO	=	0.000001

LINEAR MEASURE:
(THE UNIT IS THE METER = 39.37 INCHES)

1 CENTIMETER	=	10 MILLIMETERS	=	0.3937011	IN.
1 DECIMETER	=	10 CENTIMETERS	=	3.9370113	INS.
1 METER	=	10 DECIMETERS	=	1.0936143	YDS.
			=	3.2808429	FT.
1 DEKAMETER	=	10 METERS	=	10.936143	YDS.
1 HECTOMETER	=	10 DEKAMETERS	=	109.36143	YDS.
1 KILOMETER	=	10 HECTOMETERS	=	0.62137	MILE
1 MYRIAMETER	=	10,000 METERS			

SQUARE MEASURE:
(THE UNIT IS THE SQUARE METER = 1549.9969 SQ. INCHES)

1 SQ. CENTIMETER	= 100 SQ. MILLIMETERS	=	0.1550	SQ. IN.
1 SQ. DECIMETER	= 100 SQ. CENTIMETERS	=	15.550	SQ. INS.
1 SQ. METER	= 100 SQ. DECIMETERS	=	10.7639	SQ. FT.
1 SQ. DEKAMETER	= 100 SQ. METERS	=	119.60	SQ. YDS.
1 SQ. HECTOMETER	= 100 SQ. DEKAMETERS			
1 SQ. KILOMETER	= 100 SQ. HECTOMETERS			

(THE UNIT IS THE "ARE" = 100 SQ. METERS)

1 CENTIARE	=	10 MILLIARES	=	10.7643	SQ. FT.
1 DECIARE	=	10 CENTIARES	=	11.96033	SQ. YDS.
1 ARE	=	10 DECIARES	=	119.6033	SQ. YDS.
1 DEKARE	=	10 ARES	=	0.247110	ACRES
1 HEKTARE	=	10 DEKARES	=	2.471098	ACRES
1 SQ. KILOMETER	=	100 HEKTARES	=	0.38611	SQ. MILE

CUBIC MEASURE:
(THE UNIT IS THE "STERE" = 61,025.38659 CU. INS.)

1 DECISTERE	=	10 CENTISTERES	=	3.531562 CU. FT.
1 STERE	=	10 DECISTERES	=	1.307986 CU. YDS.
1 DEKASTERE	=	10 STERES	=	13.07986 CU. YDS.

METRIC SYSTEM

CUBIC MEASURE:
(THE UNIT IS THE METER = 39.37 INCHES)

```
1 CU. CENTIMETER = 1000 CU. MILLIMETERS  = 0.06102 CU. IN.
1 CU. DECIMETER  = 1000 CU. CENTIMETERS = 61.02374 CU. IN.
1 CU. METER      = 1000 CU. DECIMETERS  = 35.31467 CU. FT.
                 = 1 STERE              = 1.30795 CU. YDS.
1 CU. CENTIMETER (WATER)                = 1 GRAM
1000 CU. CENTIMETERS (WATER) = 1 LITER  = 1 KILOGRAM
1 CU. METER (1000 LITERS)               = 1 METRIC TON
```

MEASURES OF WEIGHT:
(THE UNIT IS THE GRAM = 0.035274 OUNCES)

```
1 MILLIGRAM  =                        =        0.015432 GRAINS
1 CENTIGRAM  = 10 MILLIGRAMS   =             0.15432 GRAINS
1 DECIGRAM   = 10 CENTIGRAMS   =             1.5432  GRAINS
1 GRAM       = 10 DECIGRAMS    =            15.4323  GRAINS
1 DEKAGRAM   = 10 GRAMS        =             5.6438  DRAMS
1 HECTOGRAM  = 10 DEKAGRAMS    =             3.5274  OUNCES
1 KILOGRAM   = 10 HECTOGRAMS   =             2.2046223 POUNDS
1 MYRIAGRAM  = 10 KILOGRAMS    =            22.046223 POUNDS
1 QUINTAL    = 10 MYRIAGRAMS   =             1.986412 CWT.
1 METRIC TON = 10 QUINTAL       = 2,2045.622      POUNDS
1 GRAM       = 0.56438 DRAMS
1 DRAM       = 1.77186 GRAMS
             = 27.3438 GRAINS
1 METRIC TON = 2,204.6223 POUNDS
```

MEASURES OF CAPACITY:
(THE UNIT IS THE LITER = 1.0567 LIQUID QUARTS)

```
1 CENTILITER = 10 MILLILITERS  =   0.338 FLUID OUNCES
1 DECILITER  = 10 CENTILITERS  =   3.38  FLUID OUNCES
1 LITER      = 10 DECILITERS   =  33.8   FLUID OUNCES
1 DEKALITER  = 10 LITERS       =   0.284 BUSHEL
1 HECTOLITER = 10 DEKALITERS   =   2.84  BUSHELS
1 KILOLITER  = 10 HECTOLITERS  = 264.2   GALLONS
```

NOTE: $\dfrac{\text{KILOMETERS}}{8} \times 5 = \text{MILES}$ or $\dfrac{\text{MILES}}{5} \times 8 = \text{KILOMETERS}$

METRIC DESIGNATOR AND TRADE SIZES

METRIC DESIGNATOR												
12	16	21	27	35	41	53	63	78	91	103	129	155
3/8	1/2	3/4	1	1 1/4	1 1/2	2	2 1/2	3	3 1/2	4	5	6
TRADE SIZE												

U.S. WEIGHTS & MEASURES / METRIC EQUIVALENT CHART

	In.	Ft.	Yd.	Mile	Mm	Cm	M	Km
1 Inch =	1	.0833	.0278	1.578×10^{-5}	25.4	**2.54**	.0254	2.54×10^{-5}
1 Foot =	12	1	.333	1.894×10^{-4}	304.8	**30.48**	.3048	3.048×10^{-4}
1 Yard =	36	3	1	5.6818×10^{-4}	914.4	91.44	**.9144**	9.144×10^{-4}
1 Mile =	63,360	5,280	1,760	1	1,609,344	160,934.4	1,609.344	**1.609344**
1 mm =	.03937	.0032808	1.0936×10^{-3}	6.2137×10^{-7}	1	0.1	0.001	0.000001
1 cm =	**.3937**	.0328084	.0109361	6.2137×10^{-6}	10	1	0.01	0.00001
1 m =	39.37	3.28084	**1.09361**	6.2137×10^{-4}	1000	100	1	0.001
1 km =	39,370	3,280.84	1,093.61	**0.62137**	1,000,000	100,000	1,000	1

In. = Inches   Ft. = Foot   Yd. = Yard   Mi. = Mile   Mm = Millimeter   Cm = Centimeter   M = Meter   Km = Kilometer

EXPLANATION OF SCIENTIFIC NOTATION:

Scientific Notation is simply a way of expressing very large or very small numbers in a more compact format. Any number can be expressed as a number between 1 & 10, multiplied by a power of 10 (which indicates the correct position of the decimal point in the original number). Numbers greater than 10 have positive powers of 10, and numbers less than 1 have negative powers of 10.

Example: $186,000 = 1.86 \times 10^{5}$ $0.000524 = 5.24 \times 10^{-4}$

USEFUL CONVERSIONS / EQUIVALENTS

1   BTU . . . . Raises 1 LB. of water 1°F
1   GRAM CALORIE . . . . . Raises 1 Gram of water 1°C
1   CIRCULAR MIL . . . . . . Equals 0.7854 sq. mil
1   SQ. MIL . . . . Equals 1.27 cir. mils
1   MIL . . . . Equals 0.001 in.

To determine circular mil of a conductor:
ROUND CONDUCTOR . . . . .CM = (Diameter in mils)^2
BUS BAR . . . . .CM = $\dfrac{\text{Width (mils)} \times \text{Thickness (mils)}}{0.7854}$

NOTES: 1 Millimeter = 39.37 Mils   1 Cir. Millimeter = 1550 Cir. Mils
           1 Sq. Millimeter = 1974 Cir. Mils

DECIMAL EQUIVALENTS

FRACTION					DECIMAL	FRACTION					DECIMAL
1/64					.0156	33/64					.5156
2/64	1/32				.0313	34/64	17/32				.5313
3/64					.0469	35/64					.5469
4/64	2/32	1/16			.0625	36/64	18/32	9/16			.5625
5/64					.0781	37/64					.5781
6/64	3/32				.0938	38/64	19/32				.5938
7/64					.1094	39/64					.6094
8/64	4/32	2/16	1/8		.125	40/64	20/32	10/16	5/8		.625
9/64					.1406	41/64					.6406
10/64	5/32				.1563	42/64	21/32				.6563
11/64					.1719	43/64					.6719
12/64	6/32	3/16			.1875	44/64	22/32	11/16			.6875
13/64					.2031	45/64					.7031
14/64	7/32				.2188	46/64	23/32				.7188
15/64					.2344	47/64					.7344
16/64	8/32	4/16	2/8	1/4	.25	48/64	24/32	12/16	6/8	3/4	.75
17/64					.2656	49/64					.7656
18/64	9/32				.2813	50/64	25/32				.7813
19/64					.2969	51/64					.7969
20/64	10/32	5/16			.3125	52/64	26/32	13/16			.8125
21/64					.3281	53/64					.8281
22/64	11/32				.3438	54/64	27/32				.8438
23/64					.3594	55/64					.8594
24/64	12/32	6/16	3/8		.375	56/64	28/32	14/16	7/8		.875
25/64					.3906	57/64					.8906
26/64	13/32				.4063	58/64	29/32				.9063
27/64					.4219	59/64					.9219
28/64	14/32	7/16			.4375	60/64	30/32	15/16			.9375
29/64					.4531	61/64					.9531
30/64	15/32				.4688	62/64	31/32				.9688
31/64					.4844	63/64					.9844
32/64	16/32	8/16	4/8	2/4	.5	64/64	32/32	16/16	8/8	4/4	1.000

Decimals are rounded to the nearest 10,000th.

TWO-WAY CONVERSION TABLE

To convert from the unit of measure in Column B to the unit of measure in Column C, multiply the number of units in Column B by the multiplier in Column A. To convert from Column C to B, use the multiplier in Column D.

EXAMPLE: To convert 1000 BTU's to CALORIES, find the "BTU - CALORIE" combination in Columns B and C. "BTU" is in Column B and "CALORIE" is in Column C; so we are converting from B to C. Therefore, we use Column A multiplier. 1000 BTU's x 251.996 = 251,996 Calories.

To convert 251,996 Calories to BTU's, use the same "BTU - CALORIE" combination. But this time you are converting from C to B. Therefore, use Column D multiplier. 251,996 Calories x .0039683 = 1,000 BTU's.

$A \times B = C$	&	$D \times C = B$
To convert from B to C, Multiply B x A:		To convert from C to B, Multiply C x D:

A	B	C	D
43,560	**Acre**	**Sq. Foot**	2.2956×10^{-5}
1.5625×10^{-3}	**Acre**	**Sq. Mile**	640
6.4516	**Ampere per sq. cm.**	**Ampere per sq. in.**	.155003
1.256637	**Ampere (turn)**	**Gilberts**	0.79578
33.89854	**Atmosphere**	**Foot of H₂0**	0.029499
29.92125	**Atmosphere**	**Inch of Hg**	0.033421
14.69595	**Atmosphere**	**Pound force/sq. in.**	0.06804
251.996	**BTU**	**Calorie**	3.96832×10^{-3}
778.169	**BTU**	**Foot-pound force**	1.28507×10^{-3}
3.93015×10^{-4}	**BTU**	**Horsepower-hour**	2544.43
1055.056	**BTU**	**Joule**	9.47817×10^{-4}
2.9307×10^{-4}	**BTU**	**Kilowatt-hour**	3412.14
3.93015×10^{-4}	**BTU/hour**	**Horsepower**	2544.43
2.93071×10^{-4}	**BTU/hour**	**Kilowatt**	3412.1412
0.293071	**BTU/hour**	**Watt**	3.41214
4.19993	**BTU/minute**	**Calorie/second**	0.23809
0.0235809	**BTU/minute**	**Horsepower**	42.4072
17.5843	**BTU/minute**	**Watt**	0.0568

| | To convert from B to C, Multiply B x A: | | To convert from C to B, Multiply C x D: |

A	B	C	D
4.1868	Calorie	Joule	.238846
0.0328084	Centimeter	Foot	30.48
0.3937	Centimeter	Inch	2.54
0.00001	Centimeter	Kilometer	100,000
0.01	Centimeter	Meter	100
6.2137×10^{-6}	Centimeter	Mile	160,934.4
10	Centimeter	Millimeter	0.1
0.010936	Centimeter	Yard	91.44
7.85398×10^{-7}	Circular mil	Sq. Inch	1.273239×10^{6}
0.000507	Circular mil	Sq. Millimeter	1973.525
0.06102374	Cubic Centimeter	Cubic Inch	16.387065
0.028317	Cubic Foot	Cubic Meter	35.31467
1.0197×10^{-3}	Dyne	Gram Force	980.665
1×10^{-5}	Dyne	Newton	100,000
1	Dyne centimeter	Erg	1
7.376×10^{-8}	Erg	Foot pound force	1.355818×10^{7}
2.777×10^{-14}	Erg	Kilowatt-hour	3.6×10^{13}
1.0×10^{-7}	Erg/second	Watt	1.0×10^{7}
12	Foot	Inch	0.0833
3.048×10^{-4}	Foot	Kilometer	3,280.84
0.3048	Foot	Meter	3.28084
1.894×10^{-4}	Foot	Mile	5,280
304.8	Foot	Millimeter	0.00328
0.333	Foot	Yard	3
10.7639	Foot candle	Lux	0.0929
0.882671	Foot of H_2O	Inch of Hg	1.13292
5.0505×10^{-7}	Foot pound force	Horsepower-hour	1.98×10^{6}
1.35582	Foot pound force	Joule	0.737562
3.76616×10^{-7}	Foot pound force	Kilowatt-hour	2.655223×10^{6}
3.76616×10^{-4}	Foot pound force	Watt-hour	2655.22
3.76616×10^{-7}	Foot pnd force/hour	Kilowatt	2.6552×10^{6}
3.0303×10^{-5}	Foot pnd force/minute	Horsepower	33,000

To convert from B to C,
Multiply B x A:

To convert from C to B,
Multiply C x D:

A	B	C	D
2.2597 x 10⁻⁵	Foot pnd force/minute	Kilowatt	44,253.7
0.022597	Foot pnd force/minute	Watt	44.2537
1.81818 x 10⁻³	Foot pnd force/second	Horsepower	550
1.355818 x 10⁻³	Foot pnd force/second	Kilowatt	737.562
0.7457	Horsepower	Kilowatt	1.34102
745.7	Horsepower	Watt	0.00134
.0022046	Gram	Pound mass	453.592
2.54 x 10⁻⁵	Inch	Kilometer	39,370
0.0254	Inch	Meter	39.37
1.578 x 10⁻⁵	Inch	Mile	63,360
25.4	Inch	Millimeter	0.03937
0.0278	Inch	Yard	36
0.07355	Inch of H₂O	Inch of Hg	13.5951
2.7777x10⁻⁷	Joule	Kilowatt-hour	3.6 X 10⁶
2.7777x10⁻⁴	Joule	Watt hour	3600
1	Joule	Watt second	1
1,000	Kilometer	Meter	0.001
0.62137	Kilometer	Mile	1.609344
1,000,000	Kilometer	Millimeter	0.000001
1,093.61	Kilometer	Yard	9.144 x 10⁻⁴
0.000621	Meter	Mile	1,609.344
1,000	Meter	Millimeter	0.001
1.0936	Meter	Yard	0.9144
1,609,344	Mile	Millimeter	6.2137 x 10⁻⁷
1,760	Mile	Yard	5.681 x 10⁻⁴
1.0936 x 10⁻³	Millimeter	Yard	914.4
0.224809	Newton	Pound force	4.44822
0.03108	Pound	Slug	32.174
0.0005	Pound	Ton (short)	2,000
0.155	Sq. Centimeter	Sq. Inch	6.4516
0.092903	Sq. Foot	Sq. Meter	10.76391
0.386102	Sq. Kilometer	Sq. Mile	2.589988

METALS

METAL	SYMB	SPEC. GRAV.	MELT POINT		ELEC. COND. % COPPER	LBS. CU. "
			C°	F°		
ALUMINUM	AL	2.71	660	1220	64.9	.0978
ANTIMONY	SB	6.62	630	1167	4.42	.2390
ARSENIC	AS	5.73	-	-	4.9	.2070
BERYLLIUM	BE	1.83	1280	2336	9.32	.0660
BISMUTH	BI	9.80	271	520	1.50	.3540
BRASS (70-30)		8.51	900	1652	28.0	.3070
BRONZE (5% SN)		8.87	1000	1832	18.0	.3200
CADMIUM	CD	8.65	321	610	22.7	.3120
CALCIUM	CA	1.55	850	1562	50.1	.0560
COBALT	CO	8.90	1495	2723	17.8	.3210
COPPER	CU					
ROLLED		8.89	1083	1981	100.0	.3210
TUBING		8.95	-	-	100.0	.3230
GOLD	AU	19.30	1063	1945	71.2	.6970
GRAPHITE		2.25	3500	6332	10^{-3}	.0812
INDIUM	IN	7.30	156	311	20.6	.2640
IRIDIUM	IR	22.40	2450	4442	32.5	.8090
IRON	FE	7.20	1200 TO 1400	2192 TO 2552	17.6	.2600
MALLEABLE		7.20	1500 TO 1600	2732 TO 2912	10	.2600
WROUGHT		7.70	1500 TO 1600	2732 TO 2912	10	.2780
LEAD	PB	11.40	327	621	8.35	.4120
MAGNESIUM	MG	1.74	651	1204	38.7	.0628
MANGANESE	MN	7.20	1245	2273	0.9	.2600
MERCURY	HG	13.65	-38.9	-37.7	1.80	.4930
MOLYBDENUM	MO	10.20	2620	4748	36.1	.3680
MONEL (63 - 37)		8.87	1300	2372	3.0	.3200
NICKEL	NI	8.90	1452	2646	25.0	.3210
PHOSPHOROUS	P	1.82	44.1	111.4	10^{-17}	.0657
PLATINUM	PT	21.46	1773	3221	17.5	.7750
POTASSIUM	K	0.860	62.3	144.1	28	.0310
SELENIUM	SE	4.81	220	428	14.4	.1740
SILICON	SI	2.40	1420	2588	10^{-5}	.0866
SILVER	AG	10.50	960	1760	106	.3790
STEEL (CARBON)		7.84	1330 TO 1380	2436 TO 2516	10	.2830
STAINLESS (18-8)		7.92	1500	2732	2.5	.2860
(13-CR)		7.78	1520	2768	3.5	.2810

METALS

METAL	SYMB	SPEC. GRAV.	MELT POINT C°	MELT POINT F°	ELEC. COND. % COPPER	LBS. CU. "
TANTALUM	TA	16.60	2900	5414	13.9	.599
TELLURIUM	TE	6.20	450	846	10⁻⁵	.224
THORIUM	TH	11.70	1845	3353	9.10	.422
TIN	SN	7.30	232	449	15.00	.264
TITANIUM	TI	4.50	1800	3272	2.10	.162
TUNGSTEN	W	19.30	3410	-	31.50	.697
URANIUM	U	18.70	1130	2066	2.80	.675
VANADIUM	V	5.96	1710	3110	6.63	.215
ZINC	ZN	7.14	419	786	29.10	.258
ZIRCONIUM	ZR	6.40	1700	3092	4.20	.231

SPECIFIC RESISTANCE (K)

THE SPECIFIC RESISTANCE (K) OF A MATERIAL IS THE RESIS-
TANCE OFFERED BY A WIRE OF THIS MATERIAL WHICH IS ONE
FOOT LONG WITH A DIAMETER OF 1 MIL.

MATERIAL	"K"	MATERIAL	"K"
BRASS	43.0	ALUMINUM	17.0
CONSTANTAN	295	MONEL	253
COPPER	10.8	NICHROME	600
GERMAN SILVER 18%	200	NICKEL	947
GOLD	14.7	TANTALUM	93.3
IRON (PURE)	60.0	TIN	69.0
MAGNESIUM	276	TUNGSTEN	34.0
MANGANIN	265	SILVER	9.7

NOTE: 1. The resistance of a wire is directly proportional to the specific
resistance of the material.
2. "K" = Specific Resistance
3. Resistance varies with temperature. See NEC, Chapter 9,
Table 8, NOTES

CENTIGRADE AND FAHRENHEIT THERMOMETER SCALES

DEG-C	DEG-F	DEG-C	DEG-F	DEG-C	DEG-F	DEG-C	DEG-F
0	32						
1	33.8	26	78.8	51	123.8	76	168.8
2	35.6	27	80.6	52	125.6	77	170.6
3	37.4	28	82.4	53	127.4	78	172.4
4	39.2	29	84.2	54	129.2	79	174.2
5	41	30	86	55	131	80	176
6	42.8	31	87.8	56	132.8	81	177.8
7	44.6	32	89.6	57	134.6	82	179.6
8	46.4	33	91.4	58	136.4	83	181.4
9	48.2	34	93.2	59	138.2	84	183.2
10	50	35	95	60	140	85	185
11	51.8	36	96.8	61	141.8	86	186.8
12	53.6	37	98.6	62	143.6	87	188.6
13	55.4	38	100.4	63	145.4	88	190.4
14	57.2	39	102.2	64	147.2	89	192.2
15	59	40	104	65	149	90	194
16	60.8	41	105.8	66	150.8	91	195.8
17	62.6	42	107.6	67	152.6	92	197.6
18	64.4	43	109.4	68	154.4	93	199.4
19	66.2	44	111.2	69	156.2	94	201.2
20	68	45	113	70	158	95	203
21	69.8	46	114.8	71	159.8	96	204.8
22	71.6	47	116.6	72	161.6	97	206.6
23	73.4	48	118.4	73	163.4	98	208.4
24	75.2	49	120.2	74	165.2	99	210.2
25	77	50	122	75	167	100	212

1. TEMP. C° = 5/9 x (TEMP. F° - 32)
2. TEMP F° = (9/5 x TEMP. C°) + 32
3. Ambient temperature is the temperature of the surrounding cooling medium.
4. Rated temperature rise is the permissible rise in temperature above ambient when operating under load.

USEFUL MATH FORMULAS

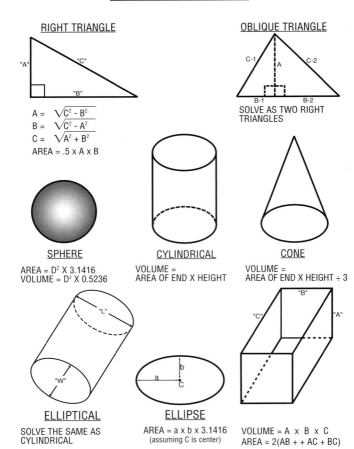

RIGHT TRIANGLE

$A = \sqrt{C^2 - B^2}$
$B = \sqrt{C^2 - A^2}$
$C = \sqrt{A^2 + B^2}$
AREA = .5 x A x B

OBLIQUE TRIANGLE

SOLVE AS TWO RIGHT TRIANGLES

SPHERE

AREA = D^2 X 3.1416
VOLUME = D^3 X 0.5236

CYLINDRICAL

VOLUME =
AREA OF END X HEIGHT

CONE

VOLUME =
AREA OF END X HEIGHT ÷ 3

ELLIPTICAL

SOLVE THE SAME AS CYLINDRICAL

ELLIPSE

AREA = a x b x 3.1416
(assuming C is center)

VOLUME = A x B x C
AREA = 2(AB + + AC + BC)

See next page for CIRCLE

THE CIRCLE

DEFINITION: A closed plane curve having every point an equal
distance from a fixed point within the curve.

CIRCUMFERENCE : The distance around a circle
DIAMETER : The distance across a circle through the center
RADIUS : The distance from the center to the edge of a circle
ARC : A part of the circumference
CHORD : A straight line connecting the ends of an arc.
SEGMENT : An area bounded by an arc and a chord
SECTOR : A part of a circle enclosed by two radii
and the arc which they cut off

CIRCUMFERENCE OF A CIRCLE = 3.1416 x 2 x Radius
AREA OF A CIRCLE = 3.1416 x Radius^2
ARC LENGTH = Degrees in arc x radius x 0.01745
RADIUS LENGTH = one half length of diameter
SECTOR AREA = one half length of arc x radius
CHORD LENGTH = 2 $\sqrt{A \times B}$
SEGMENT AREA = Sector area minus triangle area

NOTE:
3.1416 x 2 x R = 360 Degrees,
or 0.0087266 x 2 x R = 1 Degree,
or 0.01745 x R = 1 Degree
This gives us the arc formula.
DEGREES x RADIUS x 0.01745 =
    DEVELOPED LENGTH

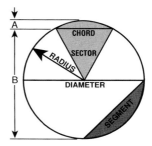

EXAMPLE:
For a ninety degree conduit bend,
having a radius of 17.25":
90 x 17.25" x 0.01745 = Developed Length
27.09" = Developed Length

FRACTIONS

DEFINITIONS:

A. A <u>FRACTION</u> is a quantity less than a unit.

B. A <u>NUMERATOR</u> is the term of a fraction indicating how many of the parts of a unit are to be taken. In a common fraction, it appears above or to the left of the line.

C. A <u>DENOMINATOR</u> is the term of a fraction indicating the number of equal parts into which the unit is divided. In a common fraction, it appears below or to the right of the line.

D. EXAMPLES:

$$(1.) \quad \frac{1}{2} \xrightarrow{\hspace{1cm}} \frac{\text{NUMERATOR}}{\text{DENOMINATOR}} = \text{FRACTION}$$

$$(2.) \quad \text{NUMERATOR} \longrightarrow \mathbf{1/2} \longleftarrow \text{DENOMINATOR}$$

TO ADD OR SUBTRACT:

TO SOLVE: 1/2 - 2/3 + 3/4 - 5/6 + 7/12 = ?

A. Determine the lowest common denominator that each of the denominators 2, 3, 4, 6, and 12 will divide into an even number of times.

The lowest common denominator is 12.

B. Work one fraction at a time using the formula:

$$\frac{\text{COMMON DENOMINATOR}}{\text{DENOMINATOR OF FRACTION}} \times \text{NUMERATOR OF FRACTION}$$

(1.) 12/2 x 1 = 6 x 1 = 6   1/2 becomes 6/12

(2.) 12/3 x 2 = 4 x 2 = 8   2/3 becomes 8/12

(3.) 12/4 x 3 = 3 x 3 = 9   3/4 becomes 9/12

(4.) 12/6 x 5 = 2 x 5 = 10   5/6 becomes 10/12

(5.) 7/12 remains 7/12

(continued next page)

FRACTIONS

TO ADD OR SUBTRACT *(CONTINUED)*:

C. We can now convert the problem from its original form to its new form using 12 as the common denominator.

$1/2 - 2/3 + 3/4 - 5/6 + 7/12 =$ Original form

$$\frac{6 - 8 + 9 - 10 + 7}{12} = \text{Present form}$$

$$\frac{4}{12} = \frac{1}{3} \quad \text{Reduced to lowest form}$$

D. To convert fractions to decimal form, simply divide the numerator of the fraction by the denominator of the fraction.

EXAMPLE: $\dfrac{1}{3} = 1$ DIVIDED BY $3 = 0.333$

TO MULTIPLY:

A. The numerator of fraction #1 times the numerator of fraction #2 is equal to the numerator of the product.

B. The denominator of fraction #1 times the denominator of fraction #2 is equal to the denominator of the product.

C. EXAMPLE:

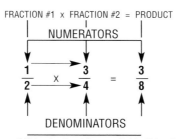

FRACTION #1 x FRACTION #2 = PRODUCT

NUMERATORS

$$\frac{1}{2} \quad \times \quad \frac{3}{4} \quad = \quad \frac{3}{8}$$

DENOMINATORS

NOTE: To change 3/8 to decimal form, divide 3 by 8 = .375

FRACTIONS

TO DIVIDE:

A. The numerator of fraction #1 times the denominator of fraction #2 is equal to the numerator of the quotient.

B. The denominator of fraction #1 times the numerator of fraction #2 is equal to the denominator of the quotient.

C. EXAMPLE: $\dfrac{1}{2} \div \dfrac{3}{4}$

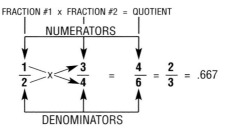

D. Alternate method for dividing by a fraction is to multiply by the reciprocal of the divisor. (the second fraction in a division problem).

E. EXAMPLE: $\dfrac{1}{2} \div \dfrac{3}{4}$

The reciprocal of $\dfrac{3}{4}$ is $\dfrac{4}{3}$

so, $\dfrac{1}{2} \div \dfrac{3}{4} = \dfrac{1}{2} \times \dfrac{4}{3} = \dfrac{4}{6} = \dfrac{2}{3} = .667$

EQUATIONS

The word "EQUATION" means equal or the same as.

A. EXAMPLE:
$$2 \times 10 = 4 \times 5$$
$$20 = 20$$

RULES:

A. **The same number may be added to both sides of an equation without changing its values.**

EXAMPLE:
$$(2 \times 10) + 3 = (4 \times 5) + 3$$
$$23 = 23$$

B. **The same number may be subtracted from both sides of an equation without changing its values.**

EXAMPLE:
$$(2 \times 10) - 3 = (4 \times 5) - 3$$
$$17 = 17$$

C. **Both sides of an equation may be divided by the same number without changing its values.**

EXAMPLE:
$$\frac{2 \times 10}{20} = \frac{4 \times 5}{20}$$
$$1 = 1$$

D. **Both sides of an equation may be multiplied by the same number without changing its values.**

EXAMPLE:
$$3 \times (2 \times 10) = 3 \times (4 \times 5)$$
$$60 = 60$$

E. **TRANSPOSITION:**
   The process of moving a quantity from one side of an equation to the other side of an equation by changing its sign of operation.

   1. **A term may be transposed if its sign is changed from plus (+) to minus (-), or from minus (-) to plus (+).**

   EXAMPLE:
$$X + 5 = 25$$
$$X + 5 - 5 = 25 - 5$$
$$X = 20$$

EQUATIONS

E. **TRANSPOSITION** (continued):

    2. **A multiplier may be removed from one side of an equation by making it a divisor in the other side; or a divisor may be removed from one side of an equation by making it a multiplier in the other side.**

    EXAMPLE: Multiplier from one side of equation (4) becomes divisor in other side.

$$4X = 40 \quad \text{becomes} \quad X = \frac{40}{4} = 10$$

    EXAMPLE: Divisor from one side of equation becomes multiplier in other side.

$$\frac{X}{4} = 10 \quad \text{becomes} \quad X = 10 \times 4$$

SIGNS:

    A. **ADDITION** of numbers with *DIFFERENT* signs:

       1. **RULE: Use the sign of the larger and subtract.**

    EXAMPLE:

$$
\begin{array}{cc}
+3 & -2 \\
+\ -2 & +\ +3 \\
\hline
+1 & +1
\end{array}
$$

    B. **ADDITION** of numbers with the *SAME* signs:

       2. **RULE: Use the common sign and add.**

    EXAMPLE:

$$
\begin{array}{cc}
+3 & -3 \\
+\ +2 & +\ -2 \\
\hline
+5 & -5
\end{array}
$$

    C. **SUBTRACTION** of numbers with *DIFFERENT* signs:

       3. **RULE: Change the sign of the subtrahend (the second number in a subtraction problem) and proceed as in addition.**

    EXAMPLE:

$$
\begin{array}{cc}
\begin{array}{c} +3 \\ -\ -2 \\ \hline \end{array} = \begin{array}{c} +3 \\ +\ +2 \\ \hline +5 \end{array}
&
\begin{array}{c} -2 \\ -\ +3 \\ \hline \end{array} = \begin{array}{c} -2 \\ +\ -3 \\ \hline -5 \end{array}
\end{array}
$$

EQUATIONS

SIGNS (continued):

D. **SUBTRACTION** of numbers with the *SAME* signs:

    4. **RULE:** Change the sign of the subtrahend (the second number in a subtraction problem) and proceed as in addition.

EXAMPLE:

$$\begin{array}{r} +3 \\ -\ +2 \\ \hline \end{array} = \begin{array}{r} +3 \\ +\ -2 \\ \hline +1 \end{array} \qquad \begin{array}{r} -3 \\ -\ -2 \\ \hline \end{array} = \begin{array}{r} -3 \\ +\ +2 \\ \hline -1 \end{array}$$

E. **MULTIPLICATION:**

    5. **RULE:** The product of any two numbers having LIKE signs is POSITIVE. The product of any two numbers having UNLIKE signs is NEGATIVE.

EXAMPLE:

$$(+3) \times (-2) = -6$$
$$(-3) \times (+2) = -6$$
$$(+3) \times (+2) = +6$$
$$(-3) \times (-2) = +6$$

F. **DIVISION:**

    6. **RULE:** If the divisor and the dividend have LIKE signs, the sign of the quotient is POSITIVE. If the divisor and dividend have UNLIKE signs, the sign of the quotient is NEGATIVE.

EXAMPLE:

$$\frac{+6}{-2} = -3 \qquad \frac{+6}{+2} = +3$$

$$\frac{-6}{+2} = -3 \qquad \frac{-6}{-2} = +3$$

NATURAL TRIGONOMETRIC FUNCTIONS

ANGLE	SINE	COSINE	TANGENT	COTANGENT	SECANT	COSECANT	
0	.0000	1.0000	.0000		1.0000		90
1	.0175	.9998	.0175	57.2900	1.0002	57.2987	89
2	.0349	.9994	.0349	28.6363	1.0006	28.6537	88
3	.0523	.9986	.0524	19.0811	1.0014	19.1073	87
4	.0698	.9976	.0699	14.3007	1.0024	14.3356	86
5	.0872	.9962	.0875	11.4301	1.0038	11.4737	85
6	.1045	.9945	.1051	9.5144	1.0055	9.5668	84
7	.1219	.9925	.1228	8.1443	1.0075	8.2055	83
8	.1392	.9903	.1405	7.1154	1.0098	7.1853	82
9	.1564	.9877	.1584	6.3138	1.0125	6.3925	81
10	.1736	.9848	.1763	5.6713	1.0154	5.7588	80
11	.1908	.9816	.1944	5.1446	1.0187	5.2408	79
12	.2079	.9781	.2126	4.7046	1.0223	4.8097	78
13	.2250	.9744	.2309	4.3315	1.0263	4.4454	77
14	.2419	.9703	.2493	4.0108	1.0306	4.1336	76
15	.2588	.9659	.2679	3.7321	1.0353	3.8637	75
16	.2756	.9613	.2867	3.4874	1.0403	3.6280	74
17	.2924	.9563	.3057	3.2709	1.0457	3.4203	73
18	.3090	.9511	.3249	3.0777	1.0515	3.2361	72
19	.3256	.9455	.3443	2.9042	1.0576	3.0716	71
20	.3420	.9397	.3640	2.7475	1.0642	2.9238	70
21	.3584	.9336	.3839	2.6051	1.0711	2.7904	69
22	.3746	.9272	.4040	2.4751	1.0785	2.6695	68
23	.3907	.9205	.4245	2.3559	1.0864	2.5593	67
24	.4067	.9135	.4452	2.2460	1.0946	2.4586	66
25	.4226	.9063	.4663	2.1445	1.1034	2.3662	65
26	.4384	.8988	.4877	2.0503	1.1126	2.2812	64
27	.4540	.8910	.5095	1.9626	1.1223	2.2027	63
28	.4695	.8829	.5317	1.8807	1.1326	2.1301	62
29	.4848	.8746	.5543	1.8040	1.1434	2.0627	61
30	.5000	.8660	.5774	1.7321	1.1547	2.0000	60
31	.5150	.8572	.6009	1.6643	1.1666	1.9416	59
32	.5299	.8480	.6249	1.6003	1.1792	1.8871	58
33	.5446	.8387	.6494	1.5399	1.1924	1.8361	57
34	.5592	.8290	.6745	1.4826	1.2062	1.7883	56
35	.5736	.8192	.7002	1.4281	1.2208	1.7434	55
36	.5878	.8090	.7265	1.3764	1.2361	1.7013	54
37	.6018	.7986	.7536	1.3270	1.2521	1.6616	53
38	.6157	.7880	.7813	1.2799	1.2690	1.6243	52
39	.6293	.7771	.8098	1.2349	1.2868	1.5890	51
40	.6428	.7660	.8391	1.1918	1.3054	1.5557	50
41	.6561	.7547	.8693	1.1504	1.3250	1.5243	49
42	.6691	.7431	.9004	1.1106	1.3456	1.4945	48
43	.6820	.7314	.9325	1.0724	1.3673	1.4663	47
44	.6947	.7193	.9657	1.0355	1.3902	1.4396	46
45	.7071	.7071	1.0000	1.0000	1.4142	1.4142	45
	COSINE	SINE	COTANGT.	TANGENT	COSECANT	SECANT	ANGLE

Note: For Angles 0 - 45, use Top Row & Left Column.
For Angles 45 - 90, use Bottom Row & Right Column

TRIGONOMETRY

TRIGONOMETRY is the mathematics dealing with the relations of sides and angles of triangles.

A **TRIANGLE** is a figure enclosed by three straight sides. The sum of the three angles is 180 degrees. All triangles have six parts: three angles and three sides opposite the angles.

RIGHT TRIANGLES are triangles that have one angle of 90 degrees and two angles of less than 90 degrees.

To help you remember the six trigonometric functions, memorize:

"OH HELL ANOTHER HOUR OF ANDY"

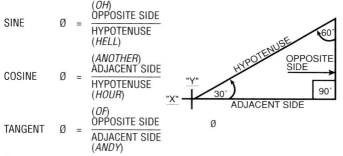

SINE   Ø   = $\dfrac{(OH)\ \text{OPPOSITE SIDE}}{\text{HYPOTENUSE}\ (HELL)}$

COSINE   Ø   = $\dfrac{(ANOTHER)\ \text{ADJACENT SIDE}}{\text{HYPOTENUSE}\ (HOUR)}$

TANGENT   Ø   = $\dfrac{(OF)\ \text{OPPOSITE SIDE}}{\text{ADJACENT SIDE}\ (ANDY)}$

Now, use backwards: **"ANDY OF HOUR ANOTHER HELL OH"**

COTANGENT Ø   = $\dfrac{(ANDY)\ \text{ADJACENT SIDE}}{\text{OPPOSITE SIDE}\ (OF)}$ Always place the angle to be solved at the vertex (where "X" and "Y" cross)

SECANT   Ø   = $\dfrac{(HOUR)\ \text{HYPOTENUSE}}{\text{ADJACENT SIDE}\ (ANOTHER)}$

COSECANT Ø   = $\dfrac{(HELL)\ \text{HYPOTENUSE}}{\text{OPPOSITE SIDE}\ (OH)}$ Note:
Ø = Theta = Any Angle

- 151 -

BENDING OFF-SETS WITH TRIGONOMETRY

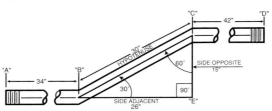

THE COSECANT OF THE ANGLE TIMES THE OFF-SET DESIRED IS EQUAL TO THE DISTANCE BETWEEN THE CENTERS OF THE BENDS.
EXAMPLE:

To make a fifteen inch (15") off-set, using thirty (30) degree bends:

1. Use Trig. Table (page 150) to find the Cosecant of a thirty (30) degree angle. We find it to be two (2).
2. Multiply two (2) times the off-set desired, which is fifteen (15) inches to determine the distance between bend "B" and bend "C". The answer is thirty (30) inches.

To mark the conduit for bending:

1. Measure from end of Conduit "A" thirty-four (34) inches to center of first bend "B", and mark.
2. Measure from mark "B" thirty (30) inches to center of second bend "C" and mark.
3. Measure from mark "C" forty-two (42) inches to "D", and mark. Cut, ream, and thread conduit before bending.

ROLLING OFF-SETS:

To determine how much off-set is needed to make a rolling off-set:

1. Measure vertical required. Use work table (any square will do) and measure from corner this amount and mark.
2. Measure horizontal required. Measure ninety degrees from the vertical line measurement (starting in same corner) and mark.
3. The diagonal distance between these marks will be the amount of off-set required.

Note: Shrink is hypotenuse minus the side adjacent.

CHICAGO-TYPE BENDERS
NINETY DEGREE BENDING

"A" to "C" = STUB-UP
"C" to "D" = TAIL
"C" = BACK OF STUB-UP
"C" = BOTTOM OF CONDUIT
Note:
There are many variations
of this type bender, but
most manufacturers
offer two sizes.
The *small* size shoe takes
1/2", 3/4" and 1" conduit.
The *large* size shoe takes
1¼" and 1½" conduit.

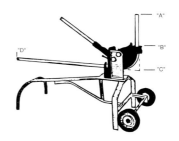

TO DETERMINE THE "TAKE-UP" AND "SHRINK" OF EACH SIZE
CONDUIT FOR A PARTICULAR BENDER TO MAKE NINETY DEGREE
BENDS:
1. Use a straight piece of scrap conduit.
2. Measure exact length of scrap conduit, "A" to "D".

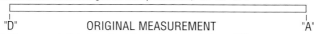

"D"   ORIGINAL MEASUREMENT   "A"

3. Place conduit in bender. Mark at edge of shoe, "B".
4. Level conduit. Bend ninety, and count number of pumps. Be sure
   to keep notes on each size conduit used.
5. After bending ninety:
   A. Distance between "B" and "C" is the TAKE-UP.
   B. Original measurement of the scrap piece of conduit subtracted
      from (distance "A" to "C" plus distance "C" to "D") is the SHRINK.
Note: Both time and energy will be saved if conduit can be cut,
        reamed and threaded before bending.

        The same method can be used on hydraulic benders.

CHICAGO-TYPE BENDERS
OFF-SETS

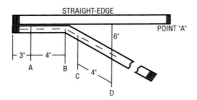

CHICAGO TYPE BENDER

EXAMPLE: To bend a 6" off-set:

1. Make a mark 3" from conduit end. Place conduit in bender with mark at outside edge of jaw.
2. Make three full pumps, making sure handle goes all the way down to the stop.
3. Remove conduit from bender and place alongside straight-edge.
4. Measure 6" from straight-edge to center of conduit. Mark point "D". Use square for accuracy.
5. Mark center of conduit from both directions through bend as shown by broken line. Where lines intersect is point "B".
6. Measure from "A" to "B" to determine distance from "D" to "C". Mark "C" and place conduit in bender with mark at outside edge of jaw, and with the kick pointing down. Use a level to prevent dogging conduit.
7. Make three full pumps, making sure handle goes all the way down to the stop.

Note: 1. There are several methods of bending rigid conduit with a Chicago Type Bender, and any method that gets the job done in a minimal amount of time with craftsmanship is acceptable.

2. Whatever method is used, quality will improve with experience.

MULTI-SHOT NINETY DEGREE CONDUIT BENDING

PROBLEM:
A. To measure, thread, cut and ream conduit before bending.
B. To accurately bend conduit to the desired height of the stub-up (H), and to the desired length of the tail (L).

GIVEN:
A. Size of conduit = 2"
B. Space between conduit (center to center) = 6"
C. Height of stub-up = 36"
D. Length of tail = 48"

SOLUTION:
A. TO DETERMINE RADIUS (R):
   Conduit #1 (inside conduit) will use the minimum radius unless otherwise specified. The minimum radius is eight times the size of the conduit. (see page 157)
   RADIUS OF CONDUIT #1 = 8 x 2" + 1.25" = 17.25"
   RADIUS OF CONDUIT #2 = RADIUS #1 + 6" = 23.25"
   RADIUS OF CONDUIT #3 = RADIUS #2 + 6" = 29.25"

B. TO DETERMINE DEVELOPED LENGTH (DL): RADIUS X 1.57 = DL
   DL OF CONDUIT #1 = R x 1.57 = 17.25" x 1.57 = 27"
   DL OF CONDUIT #2 = R x 1.57 = 23.25" x 1.57 = 36.5"
   DL OF CONDUIT #3 = R x 1.57 = 29.25" x 1.57 = 46"

C. TO DETERMINE LENGTH OF NIPPLE:
   LENGTH OF NIPPLE, CONDUIT #1 = L + H + DL - 2R
   $$= 48" + 36" + 27" - 34.5"$$
   $$= 76.5"$$
   LENGTH OF NIPPLE, CONDUIT #2 = L + H + DL - 2R
   $$= 54" + 42" + 36.5" - 46.5"$$
   $$= 86"$$
   LENGTH OF NIPPLE, CONDUIT #3 = L + H + DL - 2R
   $$= 60" + 48" + 46" - 58.5"$$
   $$= 95.5"$$

Note: 1. For 90 degree bends, SHRINK = 2R - DL
   2. For off-set bends, SHRINK = HYPOTENUSE - SIDE ADJACENT

MULTI-SHOT NINETY DEGREE CONDUIT BENDING

LAYOUT AND BENDING:

A. To locate point "B", measure from point "A", the length of the stub-up minus the radius. On all three conduit, point "B" will be 18.75" from point "A". (see page 157).

B. To locate point "C", measure from point "D", the length minus the radius, (see page 157). On all three conduit, point "C" will be 30.75" from point "D". (see page 157).

C. Divide the developed length (point "B" to point "C") into equal spaces. Spaces should not be more than 1.75" to prevent wrinkling of the conduit. On Conduit #1, seventeen spaces of 1.5882" each would give us eighteen shots of 5 degrees each. Remember there is always one less space than shot. When determining the number of shots, choose a number that will divide into ninety an even number of times.

D. If an elastic numbered tape is not available, try the method illustrated.

A to B = Conduit #1
Developed Length = 27"

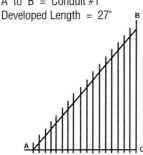

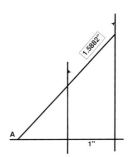

A to C = 17 1" spaces
A to B = 17 1.5882" spaces
C = table or plywood corner

Measure from Point "C" (table corner) 17 inches along table edge to Point "A" and mark. Place end of rule at Point "A". Point "B" will be located where 27" mark meets table edge B-C. Mark on board, then transfer to conduit.

MULTI-SHOT NINETY DEGREE CONDUIT BENDING

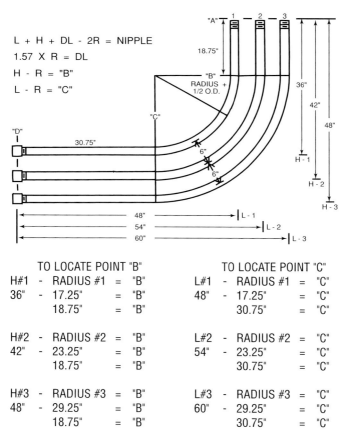

L + H + DL - 2R = NIPPLE

1.57 X R = DL

H - R = "B"

L - R = "C"

	TO LOCATE POINT "B"				TO LOCATE POINT "C"		
	H#1	-	RADIUS #1	=	"B"		L#1	-	RADIUS #1	=	"C"
	36"	-	17.25"	=	"B"		48"	-	17.25"	=	"C"
		18.75"	=	"B"			30.75"	=	"C"

Points "B" and "C" are the same distance from the end on all three
conduits.

- 157 -

OFFSET BENDS - EMT - USING HAND BENDER

An offset bend is used to change the level, or plane, of the conduit. This is usually necessitated by the presence of an obstruction in the original conduit path.

Step One:

Determine the offset depth. (X)

Step Two:

Multiply the offset depth "x" the multiplier for the degree of bend used to determine the distance between bends.

ANGLE		MULTIPLIER
10° x 10°	=	6
22½° x 22½°	=	2.6
30° x 30°	=	2
45° x 45°	=	1.4
60° x 60°	=	1.2

Example: If the offset depth required (X) is 6", and you intend to use 30° bends, the distance between bends is 6" x 2 = 12".

|← DISTANCE BETWEEN BENDS →|

Step Three:

Mark at the appropriate points, align the arrow on the bender with the first mark, and bend to desired degree by aligning EMT with chosen degree line on bender.

Step Four:

Slide down the EMT, align the arrow with the second mark, and bend to the same degree line. Be sure to note the orientation of the bender head. Check alignment.

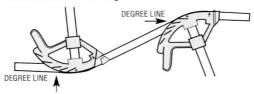

DEGREE LINE

DEGREE LINE

90° BENDS - EMT - USING HAND BENDER

The stub is the most common bend.
Step One:
    Determine the height of the stub-up required, and mark on EMT.
Step Two:
    Find the "Deduct" or "Take-up" amount from the Take-Up Chart.
    Subtract the take-up amount from the stub height, and mark the
    EMT that distance from the end.
Step Three:
    Align the arrow on bender with the last mark made on the EMT,
    and bend to the 90° mark on the bender.

DESCRIPTION		TAKE-UP
1/2" EMT	=	5"
3/4" EMT	=	6"
1" EMT	=	8"
1-1/4" EMT	=	11"

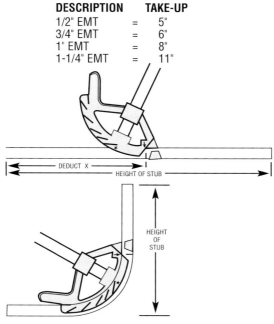

A back-to-back bend results in a "U" shape in a length of conduit. It's used for a conduit which runs along the floor or ceiling which turns up or down a wall.

Step One:

    After the first 90° bend is made, determine the back-to-back length and mark on EMT.

Step Two:

    Align this back-to-back mark with the star mark on the bender, and bend to 90°.

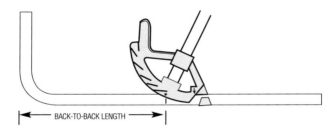

BACK-TO-BACK LENGTH

COMPLETED BEND

3-POINT SADDLE BENDS - EMT- USING HAND BENDER

The 3-point saddle bend is used when encountering an obstacle (usually another pipe)

Step One:
Measure the height of the obstruction.
Mark the center point on EMT.

Step Two:
Multiply the height of the obstruction by 2.5 and mark this distance on each side of the center mark.

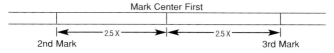

Mark Center First

2.5 X — 2.5 X

2nd Mark   3rd Mark

Step Three:
Place the center mark on the saddle mark or notch. Bend to 45°.

Step Four:
Bend the second mark to 22-1/2° angle at arrow.

Step Five:
Bend the third mark to 22-1/2° angle at arrow. Be aware of the orientation of the EMT on all bends. Check alignment.

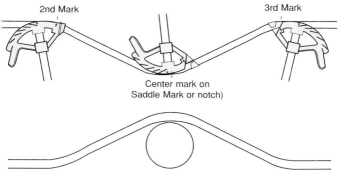

2nd Mark   3rd Mark

Center mark on
Saddle Mark or notch)

PULLEY CALCULATIONS

The most common configuration consists of a motor with a pulley attached to its shaft, connected by a belt to a second pulley. The motor pulley is referred to as the **Driving Pulley**. The second pulley is called the **Driven Pulley**. The speed at which the Driven Pulley turns is determined by the speed at which the Driving Pulley turns as well as the diameters of both pulleys. The following formulas may be used to determine the relationships between the motor, pulley diameters and pulley speeds.

D =   **Diameter of Driving Pulley**

d^1 =   **Diameter of Driven Pulley**

S =   **Speed of Driving Pulley** (revolutions per minute)

s^1 =   **Speed of Driven Pulley** (revolutions per minute)

Driving Pulley   **Driven Pulley**

- *To determine the speed of the Driven Pulley (Driven RPM):*

$$s^1 = \frac{D \times S}{d^1} \quad \text{or} \quad \text{Driven RPM} = \frac{\text{Driving Pulley Dia.} \times \text{Driving RPM}}{\text{Driven Pulley Dia.}}$$

- *To determine the speed of the Driving Pulley (Driving RPM):*

$$S = \frac{d^1 \times s^1}{D} \quad \text{or} \quad \text{Driving RPM} = \frac{\text{Driven Pulley Dia.} \times \text{Driven RPM}}{\text{Driving Pulley Dia.}}$$

- *To determine the diameter of the Driven Pulley (Driven Dia.):*

$$d^1 = \frac{D \times S}{s^1} \quad \text{or} \quad \text{Driven Dia.} = \frac{\text{Driving Pulley Dia.} \times \text{Driving RPM}}{\text{Driven RPM}}$$

- *To determine the diameter of the Driving Pulley (Driving Dia.):*

$$D = \frac{d^1 \times s^1}{S} \quad \text{or} \quad \text{Driving Dia.} = \frac{\text{Driven Pulley Dia.} \times \text{Driven RPM}}{\text{Driving RPM}}$$

USEFUL KNOTS

BOWLINE

RUNNING BOWLINE

BOWLINE ON THE BIGHT

CLOVE HITCH

SHEEPSHANK

ROLLING HITCH

SINGLE BLACKWALL HITCH

CATSPAW

DOUBLE BLACKWALL HITCH

SQUARE KNOT

TIMBER HITCH WITH HALF HITCH

SINGLE SHEET BEND

HAND SIGNALS

STOP

DOG
EVERYTHING

EMERGENCY
STOP

TRAVEL

TRAVEL
BOTH TRACKS
(CRAWLER CRANES ONLY)

TRAVEL
ONE TRACK
(CRAWLERS)

RETRACT
BOOM

EXTEND
BOOM

SWING
BOOM

HAND SIGNALS

RAISE LOAD

LOWER LOAD

MAIN HOIST

MOVE SLOWLY

RAISE BOOM AND LOWER
LOAD (FLEX FINGERS)

LOWER BOOM AND
RAISE LOAD (FLEX
FINGERS)

USE
WHIP LINE

BOOM UP

BOOM DOWN

ELECTRICAL SAFETY
DEFINITIONS
(Courtesy of Littelfuse POWR-GARD Products)

Arc-Flash - The sudden release of heat energy and intense light at the point of an arc. Can be considered a short circuit through the air, usually created by accidental contact between live conductors.

Arc-Blast - A pressure wave created by the heating, melting, vaporization, and expansion of conducting material and surrounding gases of air.

Arc Gap - The distance between energized conductors or between energized conductors and ground. Shorter arc gaps result in less energy being expended in the arc, while longer gaps reduce arc current. For 600 volts and below, arc gaps of 1.25 inches (32 mm) typically produce the maximum incident energy.

Approach Boundaries - Protection boundaries established to protect personnel from shock.

Calorie - The amount of heat needed to raise the temperature of one gram of water by one degree Celsius. 1 cal/cm^2 is equivalent to the exposure on the tip of a finger by a cigarette lighter for one second.

Distance to Arc - Refers to the distance from the receiving surface to the arc center. The value used for most calculations is typically 18 inches.

Electrically Safe Work Condition - Condition where the equipment and or circuit components have been disconnected from electrical energy sources, locked/tagged out, and tested to verify all sources of power are removed.

Exposed Live Parts - An energized conductor or part that is capable of being inadvertently touched or approached (nearer than a safe distance) by a person. It is applicable to parts that are not in an electrically safe work condition, suitably grounded, isolated, or insulated.

Flame Resistant (FR) - A term referring to fabric and its ability to limit the ignition or burning of the garment. It can be a specific characteristic of the material or a treatment applied to a material.

Reprinted with permission from Littelfuse®; www.littelfuse.com; 1-800-TEC-FUSE
For more information, refer to NFPA 70E Standards for Electrical Safety in the Workplace.

Flash Hazard Analysis - A study that analyzes potential exposure to Arc-Flash hazards. The outcome of the study establishes Incident Energy levels, Hazard Risk Categories, Flash Protection Boundaries, and required PPE. It also helps define safe work practices.

Flash Protection Boundary - A protection boundary established to protect personnel from Arc-Flash hazards. The Flash Protection Boundary is the distance at which an unprotected worker can receive a second-degree burn to bare skin.

Flash Suit - A term referring to a complete FR rated Personal Protective Equipment (PPE) system that would cover a person's body, excluding the hands and feet. Included would be pants, shirt/jacket, and flash hood with a built-in face shield.

Hazard Risk Category - A classification of risks (from 0 - 4) defined by NFPA 70E. Each category requires PPE and is related to incident energy levels.

Incident Energy - The amount of thermal energy impressed on a surface generated during an electrical arc at a certain distance from the arc. Typically measured in cal/cm^2.

PPE - An acronym for Personal Protective Equipment. It can include clothing, tools and equipment.

Qualified Person - A person who is trained and knowledgeable on the construction and operation of the equipment and can recognize and avoid electrical hazards that may be encountered.

Unqualified Person - A person that does not possess all the skills and knowledge or has not been trained for a particular task.

Shock - A trauma subjected to the body by electrical current. When personnel come in contact with energized conductors, it can result in current flowing through their body often causing serious injury or death.

Reprinted with permission from Littelfuse®; www.littelfuse.com; 1-800-TEC-FUSE
For more information, refer to NFPA 70E Standards for Electrical Safety in the Workplace.

ELECTRICAL SAFETY
CHECKLIST
(Courtesy of Littelfuse POWR-GARD Products)

1) De-energize the equipment whenever possible prior to performing any work.

2) Verify you are "qualified" and properly trained to perform the required task.

3) Identify the equipment and verify you have a clear understanding and have been trained on how the equipment operates.

4) Provide justification why the work must be performed in an "energized" condition (if applicable).

5) Identify which safe work practices will be used to insure safety.

6) Determine if a Hazard Analysis has been performed to identify all hazards (Shock, Arc-Flash, etc.).

7) Identify protection boundaries for Shock (Limited, Restricted & Prohibited Approach) and Arc-Flash (Flash Protection Boundary).

8) Identify the required Personal Protective Equipment (PPE) for the task to be performed based on the Hazard Risk Category (HRC) and available incident Energy (cal/cm^2).

9) Provide barriers or other means to prevent access to the work area by "unqualified" workers.

10) Perform a job briefing and identify job or task specific hazards.

11) Obtain written management approval to perform the work in an "energized" condition (where applicable).

ELECTRICAL SAFETY
LOCKOUT / TAGOUT PROCEDURES
(Courtesy of Littelfuse POWR-GARD Products)

OSHA requires that energy sources to machines or equipment must be turned off and disconnected isolating them from the energy source. The isolating or disconnecting means must be either locked or tagged with a warning label. While lockout is the more reliable and preferred method, OSHA accepts tagout to be a suitable replacement in limited situations. NFPA 70E Article 120 contains detailed instructions for lockout/tagout and placing equipment in an Electrically Safe Work Condition.

Application of Lockout / Tagout Devices
1. Make necessary preparations for shutdown.
2. Shut down the machine or equipment.
3. Turn OFF (open) the energy isolating device (fuse/circuit breaker).
4. Apply the lockout or tagout device.
5. Render safe all stored or residual energy.
6. Verify the isolation and deenergization of the machine or equipment.

Removal of Lockout / Tagout Devices
1. Inspect the work area to ensure that nonessential items have been removed and that machine or equipment components are intact and capable of operating properly. Especially look for tools or pieces of conductors that may have not been removed.
2. Check the area around the machine or equipment to ensure that all employees have been safely positioned or removed.
3. Make sure that only the employees who attached the locks or tags are the ones that are removing them.
4. After removing locks or tags, notify affected employees before starting equipment or machines.

Note: For specific Lockout / Tagout procedures, refer to OSHA and NFPA 70E.

Reprinted with permission from Littelfuse®; www.littelfuse.com; 1-800-TEC-FUSE

ELECTRICAL SAFETY
SHOCK PROTECTION BOUNDARIES
(Courtesy of Littelfuse POWR-GARD Products)

Nominal System Voltage (Phase to Phase)	Limited Approach Boundary		Restricted Approach Boundary	Prohibited Approach Boundary
	Exposed Fixed Circuit Part	Exposed Movable Conductor		
50 to 300 V	10 ft. 0 in.	3 ft. 6 in.	Avoid Contact	Avoid Contact
301 to 750 V	10 ft. 0 in.	3 ft. 6 in.	1 ft. 0 in.	0 ft. 1 in.
751 V to 15 kV	10 ft. 0 in.	5 ft. 0 in.	2 ft. 2 in.	0 ft. 7 in.
15.1 kV to 36 kV	10 ft. 0 in.	6 ft. 0 in.	2 ft. 7 in.	0 ft. 10 in.
36.1 kV to 46 kV	10 ft. 0 in.	8 ft. 0 in.	2 ft. 9 in.	1 ft. 5 in.
46.1 kV to 72.5 kV	10 ft. 0 in.	8 ft. 0 in.	3 ft. 2 in.	2 ft. 1 in.
72.6 kV to 121 kV	10 ft. 8 in.	8 ft. 0 in.	3 ft. 3 in.	2 ft. 8 in.

Note: Data derived from NFPA 70E Table 130.2(C)

Shock protection boundaries are based on system voltage and whether the exposed energized components are fixed or movable. NFPA 70E Table 130.2(C) defines these boundary distances for nominal phase-to-phase system voltages from 50 Volts to 800 kV. Approach Boundary distances may range from an inch to several feet. Please refer to NFPA 70E Table 130.2(C) for more information.

Protection Boundaries:

Limited Approach: Qualified person or unqualified person if accompanied by qualified person.
PPE is required.

Restricted Approach: Qualified persons only. PPE is required.

Prohibited Approach: Qualified persons only. Use PPE as if making direct contact with a live part.

ELECTRICAL SAFETY
HOW TO READ A WARNING LABEL
(Courtesy of Littelfuse POWR-GARD Products)

The amount of heat energy (cal/cm2) at the distance shown. The incident energy determines the Hazard Risk Category.

The distance from exposed energized parts at which a 2nd degree burn can occur to unprotected skin.

The NFPA 70E established Hazard Risk Category (see NFPA 70E Table 130.7(c)(11) for explanation) based on Incident Energy.

⚠ WARNING

Arc-Flash and Shock Hazard
Appropriate PPE Required

ARC-FLASH PROTECTION BOUNDARY AND REQUIRED PPE

Flash Hazard Boundary	41 inches	Hazard Risk Category	2
Incident Energy at 18" (cal/cm²)	4.05 cal/cm²	Glove Class	00

Required PPE — Cotton Underwear + FR Shirt & Pants + Safety Glasses + Hard Hat + Leather Gloves & Shoes + Ear Plugs + Face Shield

SHOCK HAZARD PROTECTION BOUNDARIES

Shock Hazard — 480 VAC

Limited 42 inches   Restricted 12 inches   Prohibited 1 inch

Equipment ID: Panel L-10   Assessment Date: 8/03/07

⚡ Littelfuse®
Expertise Applied | Answers Delivered

800-TEC-FUSE
www.littelfuse.com

Equipment voltage determining the shock approach boundaries.

Name or ID of specific electrical equipment for which this label is produced.

Required PPE (personal protective equipment) based on the Incident Energy and Hazard Risk Category.

Required glove class to protect against voltage and shock hazard.

Reprinted with permission from Littelfuse®; www.littelfuse.com; 1-800-TEC-FUSE

ELECTRICAL SAFETY
PERSONAL PROTECTION EQUIPMENT GUIDE
(Courtesy of Littelfuse POWR-GARD Products)

		Required Personal Protective Equipment (PPE), HRC 0
Hazard Risk Category 0	Minimum Arc Rating of PPE (Cal/cm²) N/A	**1 Layer** • Long Sleeve Shirt • Pants • Eye Protection • Leather Gloves

		Required Personal Protective Equipment (PPE), HRC 1
Hazard Risk Category 1	Minimum Arc Rating of PPE (Cal/cm²) 4	**1 Layer** • FR Long Sleeve Shirt • FR Pants • FR Coverall • Head Protection • Leather Protectors • Foot Protection • Eye Protection • VR Gloves

		Required Personal Protective Equipment (PPE), HRC 2
Hazard Risk Category 2	Minimum Arc Rating of PPE (Cal/cm²) 8	**1 or 2 Layers** • T-Shirt • FR Long Sleeve Shirt • FR Pants • FR Coverall • Face Shield • VR Gloves • Leather Protectors • Foot Protection • Cotton Underwear • Eye Protection • Hearing Protection • Head Protection

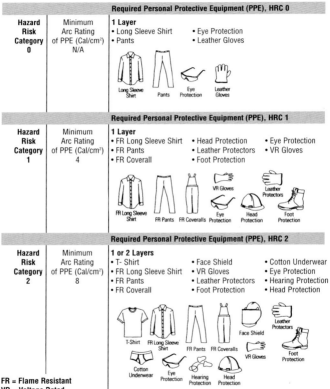

FR = Flame Resistant
VR = Voltage Rated

Disclaimer: The table above is for illustrative purposes only. PPE may vary depending on specific task. For more information refer to NFPA 70E *Standard for Electrical Safety in the Workplace*. Data derived from NFPA 70E.

Reprinted with permission from Littelfuse®; www.littelfuse.com; 1-800-TEC-FUSE

ELECTRICAL SAFETY
PERSONAL PROTECTION EQUIPMENT GUIDE
(Courtesy of Littelfuse POWR-GARD Products)

		Required Personal Protective Equipment (PPE), HRC 3		
Hazard Risk Category 3	Minimum Arc Rating of PPE (Cal/cm²) 25	**2 or 3 Layers** • T- Shirt • FR Long Sleeve Shirt • FR Pants • FR Coverall	• Flash Hood • VR Gloves • Leather Protectors • Foot Protection	• Cotton Underwear • Eye Protection • Hearing Protection • Head Protection

T-Shirt · FR Long Sleeve Shirt · FR Pants · FR Coveralls · Flash Hood · Leather Protectors · VR Gloves · Foot Protection · Cotton Underwear · Eye Protection · Hearing Protection · Head Protection

		Required Personal Protective Equipment (PPE), HRC 4		
Hazard Risk Category 4	Minimum Arc Rating of PPE (Cal/cm²) 40	**3 or more Layers** • T- Shirt • FR Long Sleeve Shirt • FR Pants • Multi-Layer Flash Suit	• Flash Hood • VR Gloves • Leather Protectors • Foot Protection	• Cotton Underwear • Eye Protection • Hearing Protection • Head Protection

T-Shirt · FR Long Sleeve Shirt · FR Pants · Flash Hood · Leather Protectors · Foot Protection · Cotton Underwear · Eye Protection · Hearing Protection · Multi-Layer Flash Suit · VR Gloves · Head Protection

FR = Flame Resistant
VR = Voltage Rated
Disclaimer: The table above is for illustrative purposes only. PPE may vary depending on specific task.
For more information refer to NFPA 70E *Standard for Electrical Safety in the Workplace.*
Data derived from NFPA 70E.

Reprinted with permission from Littelfuse® ; www.littelfuse.com; 1-800-TEC-FUSE

American Red Cross

FIRST AID

*The American Red Cross recommends certification in a CPR training
course annually and certification in a first aid course every three years.
(Also refer to author's and publisher's disclaimer on inside front cover)*

GENERAL DIRECTIONS FOR FIRST AID:
While help is being summoned, do the following:
1) CHECK - Check the scene and the injured person.
2) CALL - Call 9-1-1 or the local emergency number.
3) CARE - Care for the injured person.

URGENT CARE:
BLEEDING

First Aid:
1) Direct Pressure:
   * Place dressing and apply pressure directly over the wound,
   then elevate above the level of the heart, unless there is
   evidence of a fracture.
2) Apply pressure bandage.
   * Wrap bandage snugly over the dressing.
3) Nosebleed:
   To control a nosebleed, have the victim lean forward and
   pinch the nostrils together until bleeding stops.4) Nosebleed:
   To control a nosebleed, have the victim lean forward and
   pinch the nostrils together until bleeding stops.

POISONING

Signals: Vomiting, heavy labored breathing, sudden onset of
pain or illness, burns or odor around the lips or mouth, unusual
behavior.

First Aid:

   * If you think someone has been poisoned, call your poison control center at 1-800-222-1222 **or local emergency number and follow their directions.**

   * Try to identify the poison - be prepared to inform poison center of the type of poison, when incident occurred, victim's age, symptoms, and how much poison may have been ingested, inhaled, absorbed, or injected.

   If unconscious or nauseous:

   1) Position victim on side and monitor vital signs (i.e. pulse and breathing).

   2) Call Poison Control and identify the poison.

   3) Follow the directions of the Poison Control Center or the emergency medical services (EMS) call taker.

SHOCK

Signals: Cool, moist, pale, bluish skin, weak rapid pulse (over 100), nausea, increased rate of breathing, apathetic.

First Aid:

   Caring for shock involves the following simple steps:

   1) Have the victim lie down in the most comfortable position to minimize any pain. Pain can intensify the body's stress and accelerate the progression of shock. Help the victim to rest comfortably.

   2) Control any external bleeding

   3) Help the victim maintain normal body temperature. If the victim is cool, try to cover to avoid chill.

   4) Try to reassure the victim.

   5) Elevate the legs about 12" unless you suspect head, neck back injuries or possible broken bones involving the hips or legs. If victim is having difficulty breathing, elevate the shoulders. If unsure of the victim's condition, leave the victim lying flat.

   6) Do not give the victim anything to eat or drink.

   7) Call 911 or your local emergency number immediately.

Shock **cannot** be managed effectively by first aid alone. A victim of shock requires advanced medical care as soon as possible.

BURNS

Signals: Small or large thin (surface) burns:
redness, pain and swelling.
Deep burns: blisters, deep tissue destruction, charred
appearance.

First Aid:

1) Stop the burning - put out flames or remove the victim from the source of the burn.

2) Cool all burns - run or pour cool water on burn. Immerse if possible. Cool until pain is reduced.

3) Cover the burn - Use dry, sterile dressing and bandage.

4) Keep victim comfortable as possible, **not** chilled or over heated.

Chemical burn - must be flushed with large amounts of water until EMS arrives.

Electrical burn - make sure power is turned off before touching the victim. Care for any life-threatening conditions. Care for shock and thermal burns. Remember that anyone suffering from electric shock requires advanced medical care.

ELECTRICAL SHOCK

Signals: Unconsciousness, absence of breathing & pulse.

First Aid:

1) TURN OFF THE POWER SOURCE - Call EMS.
(DO NOT approach the victim until power has been turned off.)

2) DO NOT move a victim of electrical injury unless there is immediate danger.

3) Administer CPR if necessary.

4) Treat for shock.

5) Check for other injuries and monitor victim until Medical help arrives.

FROSTBITE

Signals: Flushed, white, yellow or blue skin. Pain. The nose, cheeks, ears, fingers, and toes are most likely to be affected. Pain may be felt early and then subside. Blisters may appear later.

First Aid:

    1) Remove wet clothing and jewelry from the affected area. *Handle the area gently. Never rub an affected area. Rubbing causes further damage to soft tissues.*

    2) Soak the frostbitten area in warm water. *Do not attempt to rewarm the frostbitten area if there is a chance that it might refreeze or if you are close to a medical facility. If you do warm the area, do so gently by soaking it in water not warmer than 105˚F. If you do not have a thermometer, test the water temperature on yourself. If the temperature is uncomfortable to your touch, it is too warm. Keep the frostbitten part in the water until normal color returns and it feels warm.*

    3) Cover with dry, sterile dressings. *Do not rub the frostbitten area. Loosely bandage the area with a dry, sterile dressing. If fingers or toes are frostbitten, place cotton or gauze between them. Do not break any blisters.*

    4) Check the ABCs, (airway, breathing, circulation), and care for shock. *Take precautions to prevent hypothermia. Call 9-1-1 or seek emergency medical help as soon as possible.*

HYPOTHERMIA

Signals: Lowered body core temperature. Persistent shivering, lips may be blue, slow slurred speech, memory lapses. Most cases occur when air temperature ranges from 30° - 50° or water temperature is below 70°F. Presence of wind and high humidity are also factors.

First Aid:

    1) Move victim to shelter and remove wet clothing if necessary.

    2) Rewarm victim with blankets or body-to-body contact in sleeping bag.

    3) If victim is conscious and able to swallow, give warm liquids.

    4) Keep victim warm and quiet.

5) DO NOT give alcoholic beverages, or beverages containing caffeine.

6) Constantly monitor victim and give CPR if necessary.

HEAT EXHAUSTION / HEAT STROKE

Signals: *Heat Exhaustion:* Pale, clammy skin, profuse perspiration, weakness, nausea, headache.

Heat Stroke: Hot dry red skin, no perspiration, rapid & weak pulse. High body temperature (105°+).

This is an immediate life threatening emergency; Call 911.

First Aid:

1) Get the victim out of the heat.

2) Loosen tight clothing or restrictive clothing.

3) Remove perspiration soaked clothing.

4) Apply cool, wet cloths to the skin.

5) Fan the victim.

6) If victim is conscious, give cool water to drink.

7) Call for an ambulance if victim refuses water, vomits, or starts to lose consciousness.

FIRST AID FOR CHOKING

If the person cannot cough, speak or breathe:

When an adult is choking:

Step 1: **CHECK** scene, then **CHECK** person.

Step 2: Have someone **CALL 9-1-1**.

Step 3: Obtain consent.

Step 4: Lean the person forward and give 5 back blows with the heal of your hand.

Step 5: Give 5 quick, upward abdominal thrusts.

To give abdominal thrusts, *stand behind the person and wrap your arms around his or her waist. Make a fist with one hand and place the thumb side against the middle of the person's abdomen, just above the navel and well below the* *lower tip of the breastbone. Grab your fist with your other hand and give quick, upward thrusts into the abdomen. Each back blow and abdominal thrust should be a separate and distinct attempt to dislodge the obstruction.*

(**Note:** Give chest thrusts to a choking person who is pregnant or too big for you to reach around.)

(**Note:** You can give yourself abdominal thrusts by using your hands, just as you would do to another person, or lean over and press your abdomen against any firm object such as the back of a chair.)

Step 6: Continue back blows and abdominal thrusts until -
- Object is forced out.
- Person can breathe or cough forcefully.
- Person becomes unconscious.

Note: If the person becomes unconscious, CALL 9-1-1, if not already done.

Disaster Preparedness

Be Prepared To Save A Life

**Be prepared for an
accident with an
American Red Cross
Family First Aid Kit.**

The **American Red Cross Family First Aid Kit** makes
it easy to treat almost any emergency quickly and correctly.

The kit contains sealed packets and printed step-by-step
directions and is ideal for easy storage. Count on the Red
Cross to back you up with a complete line of first aid kits for
your car, home, truck or workplace.

For more information contact your local Red Cross
chapter. In Houston, Texas and surrounding counties, call
1**(866) 526-8300**.

**Now you'll be
prepared, when
it's up to you.**

*The American Red Cross recommends CPR certification annually
and first aid certification every three years.*

www.houstonredcross.org

2008 CALENDAR

JANUARY

S	M	T	W	T	F	S
		1	2	3	4	5
6	7	8	9	10	11	12
13	14	15	16	17	18	19
20	21	22	23	24	25	26
27	28	29	30	31		

FEBRUARY

S	M	T	W	T	F	S
					1	2
3	4	5	6	7	8	9
10	11	12	13	14	15	16
17	18	19	20	21	22	23
24	25	26	27	28	29	

MARCH

S	M	T	W	T	F	S
						1
2	3	4	5	6	7	8
9	10	11	12	13	14	15
16	17	18	19	20	21	22
23	24	25	26	27	28	29
30	31					

APRIL

S	M	T	W	T	F	S
		1	2	3	4	5
6	7	8	9	10	11	12
13	14	15	16	17	18	19
20	21	22	23	24	25	26
27	28	29	30			

MAY

S	M	T	W	T	F	S
				1	2	3
4	5	6	7	8	9	10
11	12	13	14	15	16	17
18	19	20	21	22	23	24
25	26	27	28	29	30	31

JUNE

S	M	T	W	T	F	S
1	2	3	4	5	6	7
8	9	10	11	12	13	14
15	16	17	18	19	20	21
22	23	24	25	26	27	28
29	30					

JULY

S	M	T	W	T	F	S
		1	2	3	4	5
6	7	8	9	10	11	12
13	14	15	16	17	18	19
20	21	22	23	24	25	26
27	28	29	30	31		

AUGUST

S	M	T	W	T	F	S
					1	2
3	4	5	6	7	8	9
10	11	12	13	14	15	16
17	18	19	20	21	22	23
24	25	26	27	28	29	30
31						

SEPTEMBER

S	M	T	W	T	F	S
	1	2	3	4	5	6
7	8	9	10	11	12	13
14	15	16	17	18	19	20
21	22	23	24	25	26	27
28	29	30				

OCTOBER

S	M	T	W	T	F	S
			1	2	3	4
5	6	7	8	9	10	11
12	13	14	15	16	17	18
19	20	21	22	23	24	25
26	27	28	29	30	31	

NOVEMBER

S	M	T	W	T	F	S
						1
2	3	4	5	6	7	8
9	10	11	12	13	14	15
16	17	18	19	20	21	22
23	24	25	26	27	28	29
30						

DECEMBER

S	M	T	W	T	F	S
	1	2	3	4	5	6
7	8	9	10	11	12	13
14	15	16	17	18	19	20
21	22	23	24	25	26	27
28	29	30	31			

2009 CALENDAR

JANUARY
S	M	T	W	T	F	S
				1	2	3
4	5	6	7	8	9	10
11	12	13	14	15	16	17
18	19	20	21	22	23	24
25	26	27	28	29	30	31

FEBRUARY
S	M	T	W	T	F	S
1	2	3	4	5	6	7
8	9	10	11	12	13	14
15	16	17	18	19	20	21
22	23	24	25	26	27	28

MARCH
S	M	T	W	T	F	S
1	2	3	4	5	6	7
8	9	10	11	12	13	14
15	16	17	18	19	20	21
22	23	24	25	26	27	28
29	30	31				

APRIL
S	M	T	W	T	F	S
			1	2	3	4
5	6	7	8	9	10	11
12	13	14	15	16	17	18
19	20	21	22	23	24	25
26	27	28	29	30		

MAY
S	M	T	W	T	F	S
					1	2
3	4	5	6	7	8	9
10	11	12	13	14	15	16
17	18	19	20	21	22	23
24	25	26	27	28	29	30
31						

JUNE
S	M	T	W	T	F	S
	1	2	3	4	5	6
7	8	9	10	11	12	13
14	15	16	17	18	19	20
21	22	23	24	25	26	27
28	29	30				

JULY
S	M	T	W	T	F	S
			1	2	3	4
5	6	7	8	9	10	11
12	13	14	15	16	17	18
19	20	21	22	23	24	25
26	27	28	29	30	31	

AUGUST
S	M	T	W	T	F	S
						1
2	3	4	5	6	7	8
9	10	11	12	13	14	15
16	17	18	19	20	21	22
23	24	25	26	27	28	29
30	31					

SEPTEMBER
S	M	T	W	T	F	S
		1	2	3	4	5
6	7	8	9	10	11	12
13	14	15	16	17	18	19
20	21	22	23	24	25	26
27	28	29	30			

OCTOBER
S	M	T	W	T	F	S
				1	2	3
4	5	6	7	8	9	10
11	12	13	14	15	16	17
18	19	20	21	22	23	24
25	26	27	28	29	30	31

NOVEMBER
S	M	T	W	T	F	S
1	2	3	4	5	6	7
8	9	10	11	12	13	14
15	16	17	18	19	20	21
22	23	24	25	26	27	28
29	30					

DECEMBER
S	M	T	W	T	F	S
		1	2	3	4	5
6	7	8	9	10	11	12
13	14	15	16	17	18	19
20	21	22	23	24	25	26
27	28	29	30	31		

2 0 1 0 CALENDAR

JANUARY

S	M	T	W	T	F	S
					1	2
3	4	5	6	7	8	9
10	11	12	13	14	15	16
17	18	19	20	21	22	23
24	25	26	27	28	29	30
31						

FEBRUARY

S	M	T	W	T	F	S
	1	2	3	4	5	6
7	8	9	10	11	12	13
14	15	16	17	18	19	20
21	22	23	24	25	26	27
28						

MARCH

S	M	T	W	T	F	S
	1	2	3	4	5	6
7	8	9	10	11	12	13
14	15	16	17	18	19	20
21	22	23	24	25	26	27
28	29	30	31			

APRIL

S	M	T	W	T	F	S
				1	2	3
4	5	6	7	8	9	10
11	12	13	14	15	16	17
18	19	20	21	22	23	24
25	26	27	28	29	30	

MAY

S	M	T	W	T	F	S
						1
2	3	4	5	6	7	8
9	10	11	12	13	14	15
16	17	18	19	20	21	22
23	24	25	26	27	28	29
30	31					

JUNE

S	M	T	W	T	F	S
		1	2	3	4	5
6	7	8	9	10	11	12
13	14	15	16	17	18	19
20	21	22	23	24	25	26
27	28	29	30			

JULY

S	M	T	W	T	F	S
				1	2	3
4	5	6	7	8	9	10
11	12	13	14	15	16	17
18	19	20	21	22	23	24
25	26	27	28	29	30	31

AUGUST

S	M	T	W	T	F	S
1	2	3	4	5	6	7
8	9	10	11	12	13	14
15	16	17	18	19	20	21
22	23	24	25	26	27	28
29	30	31				

SEPTEMBER

S	M	T	W	T	F	S
			1	2	3	4
5	6	7	8	9	10	11
12	13	14	15	16	17	18
19	20	21	22	23	24	25
26	27	28	29	30		

OCTOBER

S	M	T	W	T	F	S
					1	2
3	4	5	6	7	8	9
10	11	12	13	14	15	16
17	18	19	20	21	22	23
24	25	26	27	28	29	30
31						

NOVEMBER

S	M	T	W	T	F	S
	1	2	3	4	5	6
7	8	9	10	11	12	13
14	15	16	17	18	19	20
21	22	23	24	25	26	27
28	29	30				

DECEMBER

S	M	T	W	T	F	S
			1	2	3	4
5	6	7	8	9	10	11
12	13	14	15	16	17	18
19	20	21	22	23	24	25
26	27	28	29	30	31	

GENERAL ALPHABETICAL INDEX

GENERAL ALPHABETICAL INDEX

- Detach along perforations -

UGLY'S 2008 REGISTRATION CARD

Please enter my name into your UGLY'S database, and contact me with information on new UGLY'S products/updates as they become available.

I understand that UGLY'S will not share my personal information with any other parties.

Name: _____

Company Name: (if purchased in name of company) _____

Mailing Address: _____

City: _____ State: _____ Zip: _____

Phone: (_____) _____ ext.: _____ Fax: (_____) _____

E-mail address: _____

Please check the box that best describes your job function:

☐ Electrical Contractor ☐ Engineering/Design ☐ Plant/Facilities ☐ Maintenance/Repair
☐ Instructor ☐ Student ☐ Other _____

Please check the box that best describes how you acquired this UGLY'S product:

☐ Electrical Supply Co. ☐ Bookstore ☐ Burleson Distributing ☐ Gift
☐ Other _____

02

BURLESON DISTRIBUTING CORPORATION
3501 OAK FOREST DRIVE
HOUSTON, TX 77018-6121